Think Like a Street Photographer

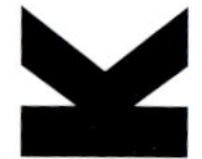

First published in Great Britain in 2021
by Laurence King, an imprint of
The Orion Publishing Group Ltd
Carmelite House, 50 Victoria Embankment
London EC4Y 0DZ

An Hachette UK Company

The authorised representative in the EEA
is Hachette Ireland, 8 Castlecourt Centre,
Dublin 15, D15 XTP3, Ireland (email: info@hbgi.ie)

10 9 8

A catalogue record for this book
is available from the British Library.

ISBN: 978 1 78627 728 2

Design: Florian Michelet
Origination by DL Imaging Ltd
Printed in China by C&C Offset Printing Co Ltd

www.laurenceking.com
www.orionbooks.co.uk

Think Like a Street Photographer

Laurence King

Matt Stuart

FOREWORD

Matt's photography appears, at first, to document another world: some place populated by extraordinary characters and coincidences; separated from time, and placed before our gaze to sparkle and fizz. He lifts a veil of drabness from the world to disclose unfamiliar, arresting moments. Turning the pages of this book, we bounce from one improbably fortuitous moment to another, and wonder where these costumed devils, lively balloons and gargantuan peacocks hide away when we go in search of our own street photography

Matt and I both strive to create wonder through forms of magic, to tell a story about reality. I am known in my pocket of the world as a mentalist, a kind of magician; on stage I read minds and on TV I take unwitting participants through psychological experiments. Both street photographer and magician exploit the human desire to edit complex reality into a neat narrative – the same narrative we then mistake for objectivity.

A magician cajoles us into recalling the story of the trick in an edited way: we delete certain parts of what happened, join up the wrong dots and remember the trick as the magician wished. Likewise, a photographic moment of time, lifted from the free-flow of reality and presented within a frame, is an exercise in preferential editing that tickles our urge to create a story from limited data. We don't see what a magician does during the moments we aren't looking or thinking straight enough; likewise, we are at the mercy of a photograph because it delineates and controls its story. In each case, the effect relies on a masterful control of the audience's attention and focus.

There is an enchanted place where Matt's work meets magic. In his photographs, we have a series of 'unlikelihoods' that suggest Matt walks different streets from us. Likewise, magic bestows upon the performer a special aura. And yet there is a phrase in magic – coined by Jim Steinmeyer, a great creator of magical illusions –

that 'a magician guards an empty safe'. What he means is that we jealously protect the secrets of our craft not because they are dangerous and exciting, but because they are almost always silly and disappointing. Thus, the discrepancy between the *effect* and the *method* makes the field of magic an excellent example of the deceptive nature of what is often called 'talent'. Matt abhors the word, seeing talent as an illusion created only by repeated, even mundane, hard work. As is clear from these pages, it is his relentless application of craft, unalloyed positivity and his singular perspective that elevate his work into art and conjure this witty, compelling, parallel universe.

Tenacity is Matt's trick. And an ability to be tenacious is what he seeks to inspire.

This book, then, is a call for us to keep going, to keep making pictures and keep thinking about how we're making them, because the luck that Matt seems to harness, almost supernaturally, comes principally from hard work. The illusion may be magical, but the means are earthly: maximize your opportunities and the universe will provide. To be tenacious, we need to love what we do, and find new ways of loving it.

When I first met Matt, we spoke about an eternal problem: the furtive awkwardness involved in photographing in the street. He told me that if he feels guilty taking pictures, people are more likely to take offence. When, however, he *meets those people with love*, he contends with far less objection, and somehow more images 'arrive'. In person, Matt is light and buoyant, and seems infused with a positive and focused energy that must help his project. For those of us lumbered with awkward diffidence, we can only learn from him and do our best.

It is not another world that Matt captures, it is our own. It is the one that greets us every day and holds us within it, and there is so much more to see than meets the eye.

Derren Brown, 2020

CONTENTS

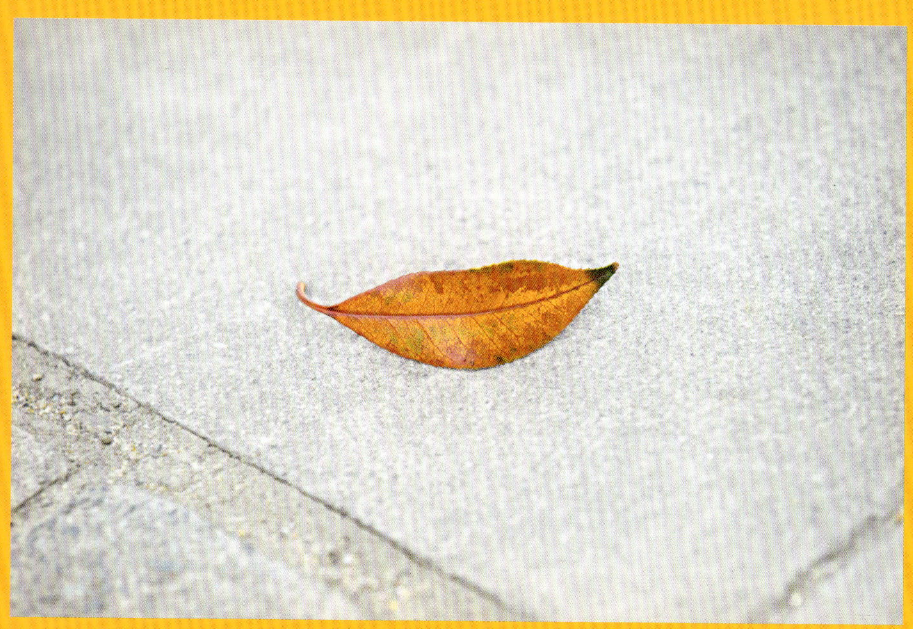

Wrentham Avenue, London, 2013

Chapter 1

THINK LUCKY, BE LUCKY

A positive mental attitude is the key to great pictures

Going out into the world to make pictures can be overwhelming. It's all a great big unknown. If you put too much pressure on yourself to make 'great' pictures, you can become paralysed, so give yourself an optimistic push and have hope.

A positive mental attitude is the key to great photographs. If you go out expecting to see interesting pictures, you tend to be more positive, and then luckier. As the great photographer and curator John Szarkowski said: 'Luck is the attentive photographer's best teacher.' My general outlook is, get up, get out and go and find things. I try to summon an excitement and amazement for life.

Luck is about switching on your eyes and your head, but, at the risk of sounding sentimental, you do have to switch on your heart – your *love* for things. Love is

'A positive mental attitude is the key to great photographs. If you go out expecting to see interesting pictures, you tend to be more positive, and then luckier.'

a word I don't like using too much because it's bandied around all the time, but it's helpful to engage your empathy and feel an affinity for what you're looking at. Ultimately, you need to remember how lucky you are to be walking around with a strange black box looking at things, making a record of them and bringing them home. It's a privilege.

Having a positive disposition is necessary for this activity that we call street photography because, to quote photographer Alex Webb, 'street photography is 99.9 per cent about failure'. Here's an extract from his fantastic book *On Street Photography and the Poetic Image* (with co-author Rebecca Norris Webb), which points to the mental fortitude every street photographer must develop and practise: 'So often I feel defeated by the street. I sometimes find, however, that if I keep walking, keep looking, and keep pushing myself, eventually something interesting will happen ... Every once in a while, at the end of the day, when I'm most exhausted and hungry, something – a shaft of light, an unexpected gesture, an odd juxtaposition – suddenly reveals a photograph.'

Even if you're not a natural optimist, it's possible to trick yourself into having a positive outlook. *Will* yourself lucky. Develop a mantra: 'I will be lucky, I will be lucky, I will be lucky.' I'm a great believer in making your own luck. My friend, photographer Blake Andrews, once said, 'If you don't expect to see good photos, you won't. If you expect to find them, they are everywhere.'

There will be times, inevitably, when you can't quite get the engine going, and that's OK. It's important to understand that some days are good and others are bad; but on the days that you want to be good, you're going out with your head held high and will embrace everything you see, from a crack in the pavement to a leaf that looks like a smile.

TRY THIS

Don't be reluctant to press the button,
even if the picture is not quite there.
Saying 'yes' and keeping yourself
'awake' will stop any overthinking.

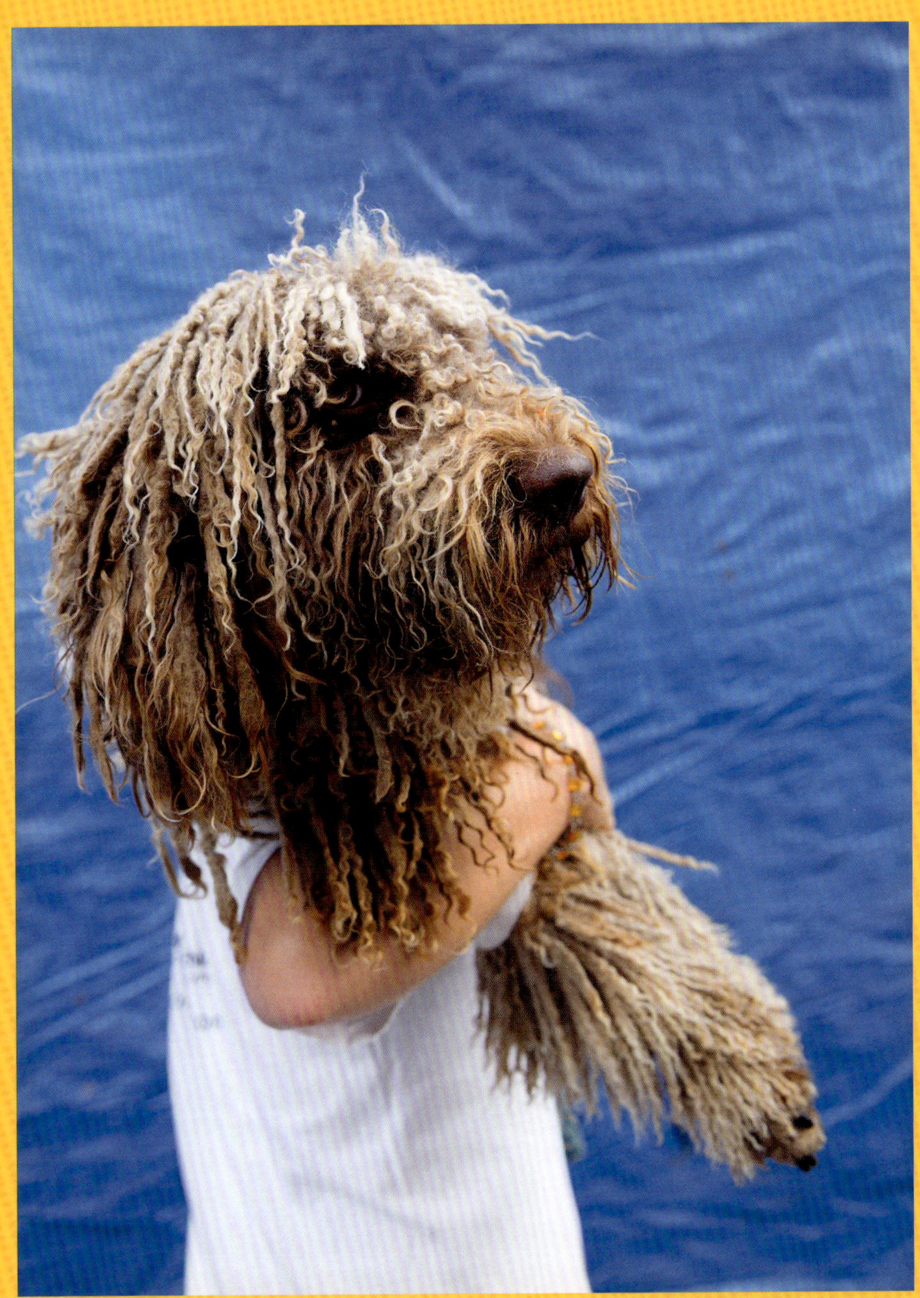

Buñol, Spain, 2017

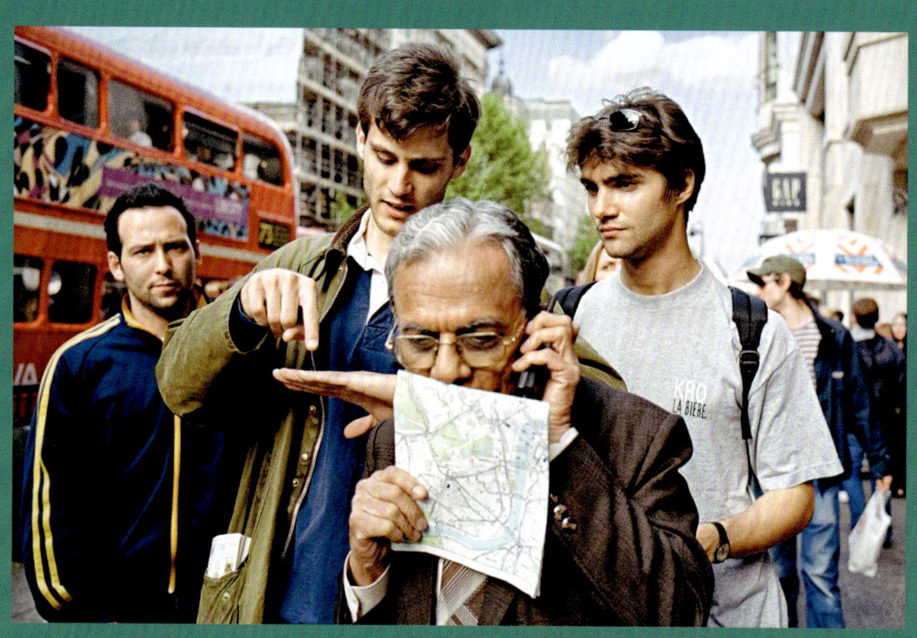

Oxford Circus, London, 2005

Chapter 2

GET INTO THE FLOW

Find yourself and get lost

Being out on the street making pictures is a time to be in your head.
It's a chance to leave everything else behind. In one sense,
you are absorbed by what you're doing, but at the same time you're
totally aware of what's happening, tuned in and switched on.

There's a sense of finding your flow, your rhythm – getting into your stride, so to speak – when you're out on the street taking photographs, and, as a person who has spent most of his life pounding pavements, first as a BMXer and skateboarder and then as a photographer, I've learned to become attuned with the great unknown that is street life.

I have three different levels of engagement when I'm out photographing. The first is to do with being 'on patrol' – surveying the scene, getting a sense of what's happening. The second is being involved, but not fully tuned in. And the third is being totally switched on and completely tuned

'There's a sense of finding your flow, your rhythm – getting into your stride, so to speak – when you're out on the street taking photographs.'

in to glances, gestures, expressions and feelings. In this state, I forget everything else. I tend to dip in and out of these states of consciousness, but if I see something that catches my interest, I fast-track to level three.

Students attending my workshops sometimes ask if it's a good idea to get yourself lost – as in, put yourself in a place with which you're unfamiliar. This might lead to good pictures, but you need to know in advance whether the place you're in is likely to deliver or not. By this I mean, does it seem as if there will be lots of opportunities to make pictures? Developing a sense of how and why a place is 'good' comes from spending a lot of time there, scoping it out and repeatedly photographing there. Oxford Circus, in the heart of London, is one such place for me – it's a place I've been photographing on and off for more than 20 years. While I advocate wandering about and finding new places, it can be helpful to understand the territory in which you are photographing – the hotspots as well as the places that are less fruitful.

Sometimes I am asked if wearing headphones is a good way to get into the zone, and a quote from the Swiss-American photographer Robert Frank springs to mind: 'The eye should learn to listen before it looks.' If you wear headphones, there is a danger you will miss things. Most of the time you hear something that is happening *before* you see it, so I don't recommend the headphone experience. You need to be alert.

Wandering around with your camera may feel like you're not doing anything, but being out 'doing nothing' can be a very active time. Every time you go out, you learn a little more about putting yourself in places where you can get good pictures and why one thing is more likely to make a good picture than another. Give yourself that time to go out and look, because as well as looking, you will also feel, and feeling is a very important part of the process too – how you respond not just physically but mentally.

TRY THIS

Turn your back on the event and focus on the crowd. As the great photographer Elliott Erwitt said: 'After following the crowd for a while, I'd then go 180 degrees in the exact opposite direction. It always worked for me.'

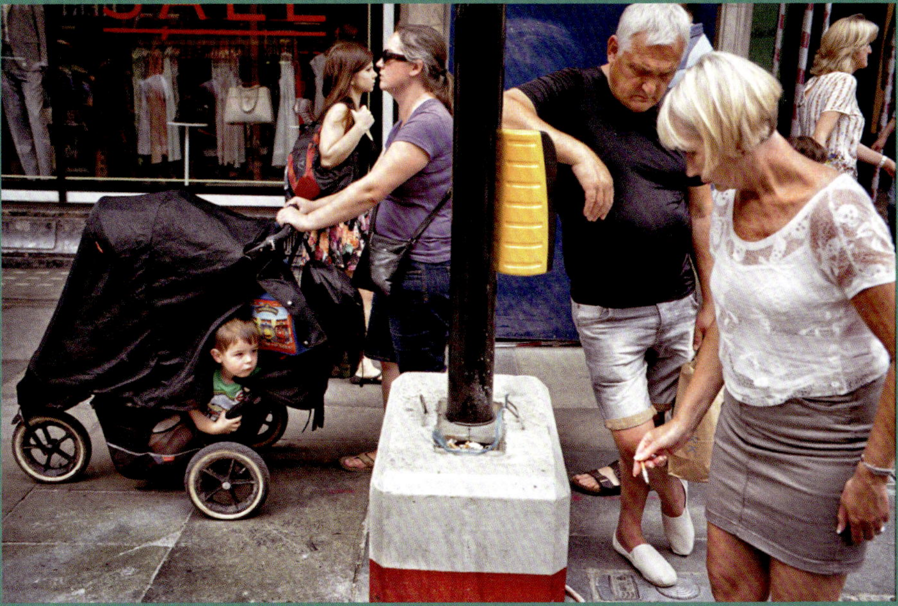

Regent Street, London, 2015

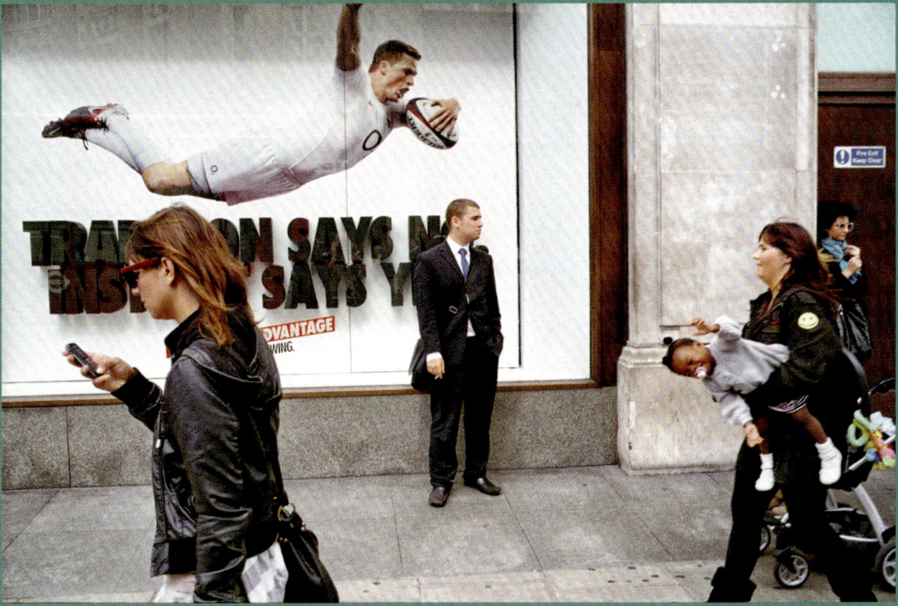

Oxford Circus, London, 2011

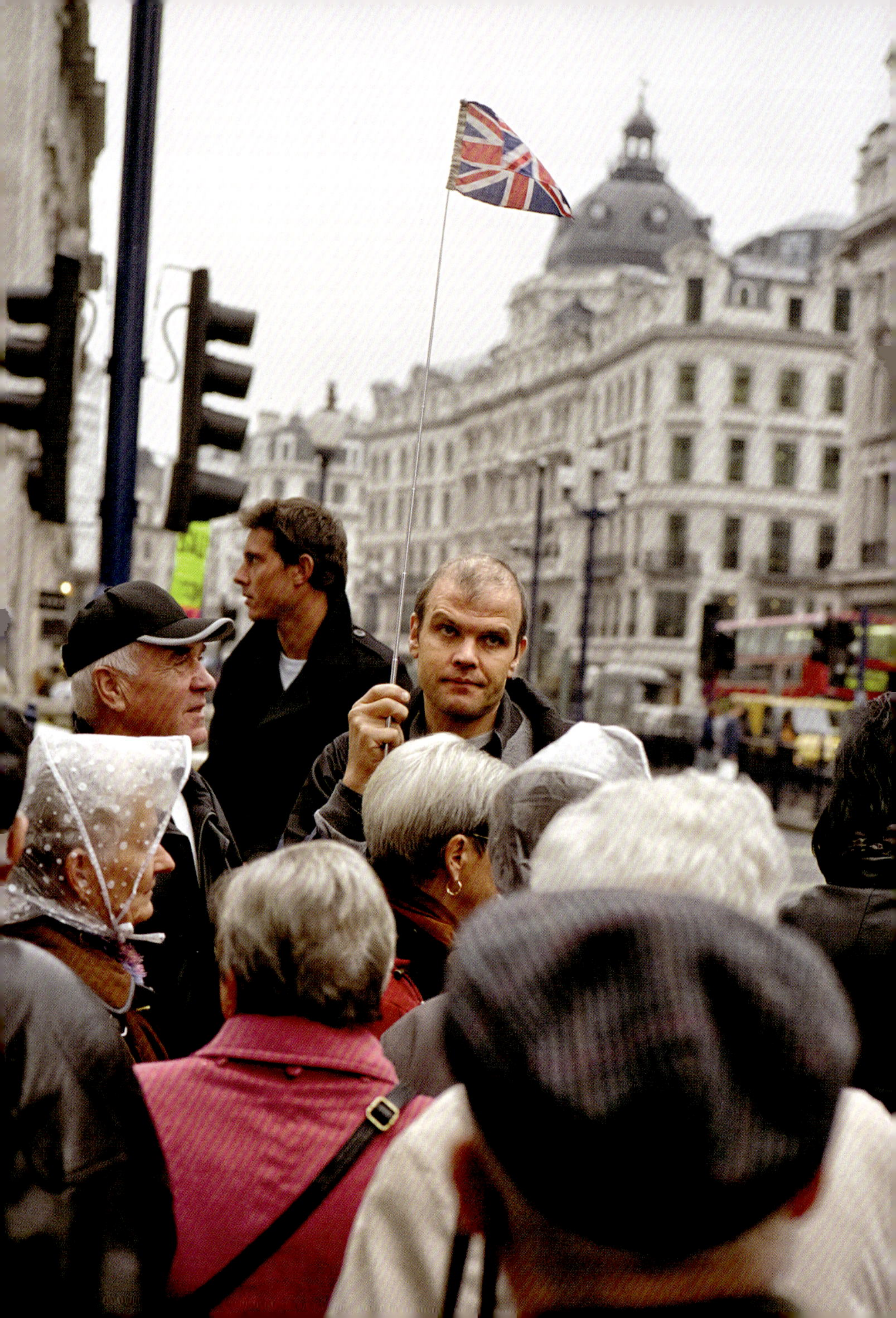

Chapter 3

BAD WEATHER, GOOD PHOTOS

Don't be a fair-weather photographer

Always carry a camera with you – on good weather days, rainy days, snowy days, windy days – because you never know what might come your way.

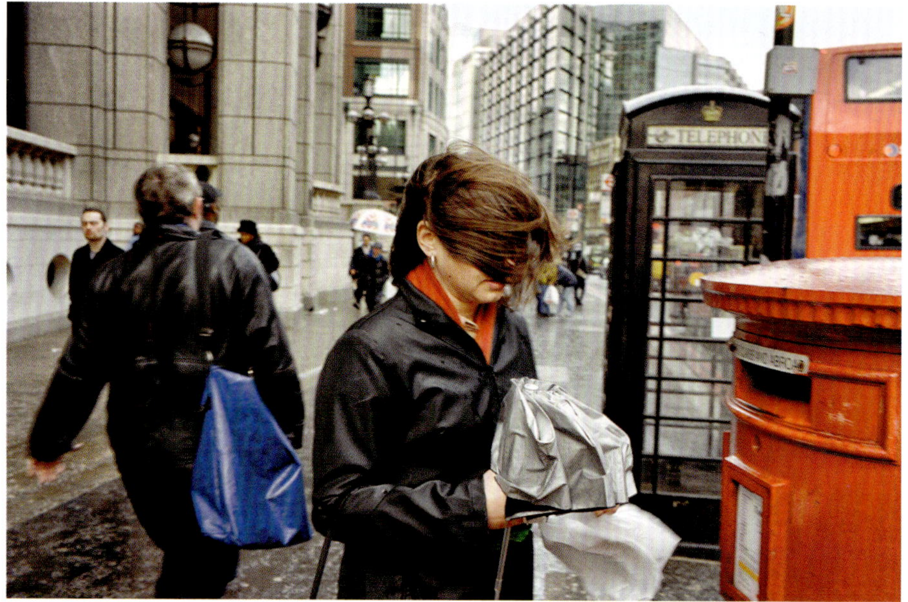

Page 16 Broadgate, London, 2007   **Above** Oxford Circus, London, 2006

When early-morning sun pours through your window it's not difficult to summon the energy to grab your camera and get outside. But on days when the weather is less than desirable, doing such a thing becomes much more of a challenge. Yet in truth, there is no such thing as a bad-weather day because even on rainy or blustery days, there's a chance that pictures will come your way.

Some of the best pictures come about when it's raining because people do funny things, like cover their head with a newspaper in a futile attempt to keep dry, or huddle under an overhang and peer out every so often, willing the rain to subside so they can continue on their way. You never know what's around the next corner, even when the weather is bad.

The day I made the picture of a dog that appears to be out having a nice time in a car (pages 20-21) is a case in point. I was living in London's Barbican estate at the time; it was a Sunday, it was raining and I was hungover. In dire need of some Alka-Seltzer, I dragged myself up and shuffled out through the Barbican tunnel onto Aldersgate Street, towards the chemist. Before I left, I somehow remembered to pick up my small camera. I was pretty certain nothing was going to happen, although who knew? I went to cross the road and at the traffic lights, on a rainy day, there was a convertible car with the roof down. In the back of the car (although it looked like the front), was a Great Dane – the greatest Great Dane I've ever seen. It was sitting there proudly, slightly looking down its nose at me as I crossed the road.

I quickly went for my pocket, pulled out my camera and moved to the front of the car, snapping two or three pictures. The people in the car looked at me in surprise, so I said, 'I love your dog!' They said, 'Thank you very much.' And off I went to get my Alka-Seltzer, not quite sure whether I was still drunk and had hallucinated the whole encounter.

I put the film into the lab the following day, because at that time, when I still used film, I didn't delay in getting it developed; I'm impatient and wanted to know

'If you don't have a camera on you at all times... you're just someone who saw some stuff and told people about what you saw.'

whether I'd got the shot or not. When I got the film back, I saw I had this picture of the Great Dane looking like it's driving a convertible car. The dog had probably been photographed thousands of times and was, I imagine, extremely used to it. The picture was used in a portfolio for the *Guardian* newspaper about six months later.

About a week after the picture was published, I got a call from the dog's owners. It's always a little unnerving when someone gets in touch saying, 'Hello, did you take such and such a picture?' because you think, 'Uh oh, where is this going?' I replied that I had indeed taken it and they asked whether it would be possible to get a print because they liked it so much and because Joe, the dog, had died. It was no problem to send a print, I said, and so, in a nice but also sad way, we reconnected, and Joe the greatest Great Dane has been immortalized.

So the moral of the story is always to carry a camera with you – on good-weather days, rainy days, snowy days, windy days, *every* day, because you never know what might come your way. If you don't have a camera on you at all times, you're not really a photographer; you're just someone who saw some stuff and told people about what you saw.

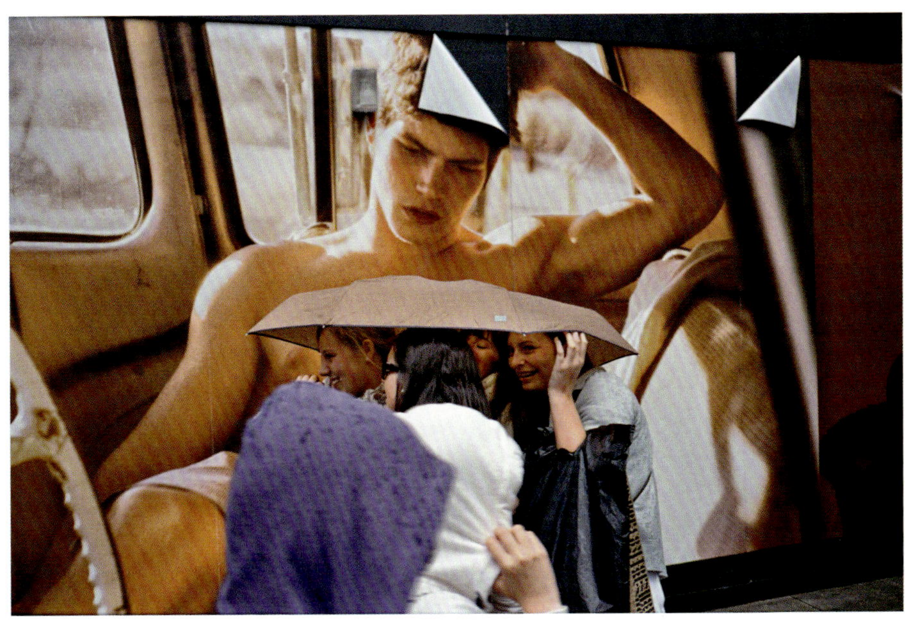

Oxford Street, London, 2008

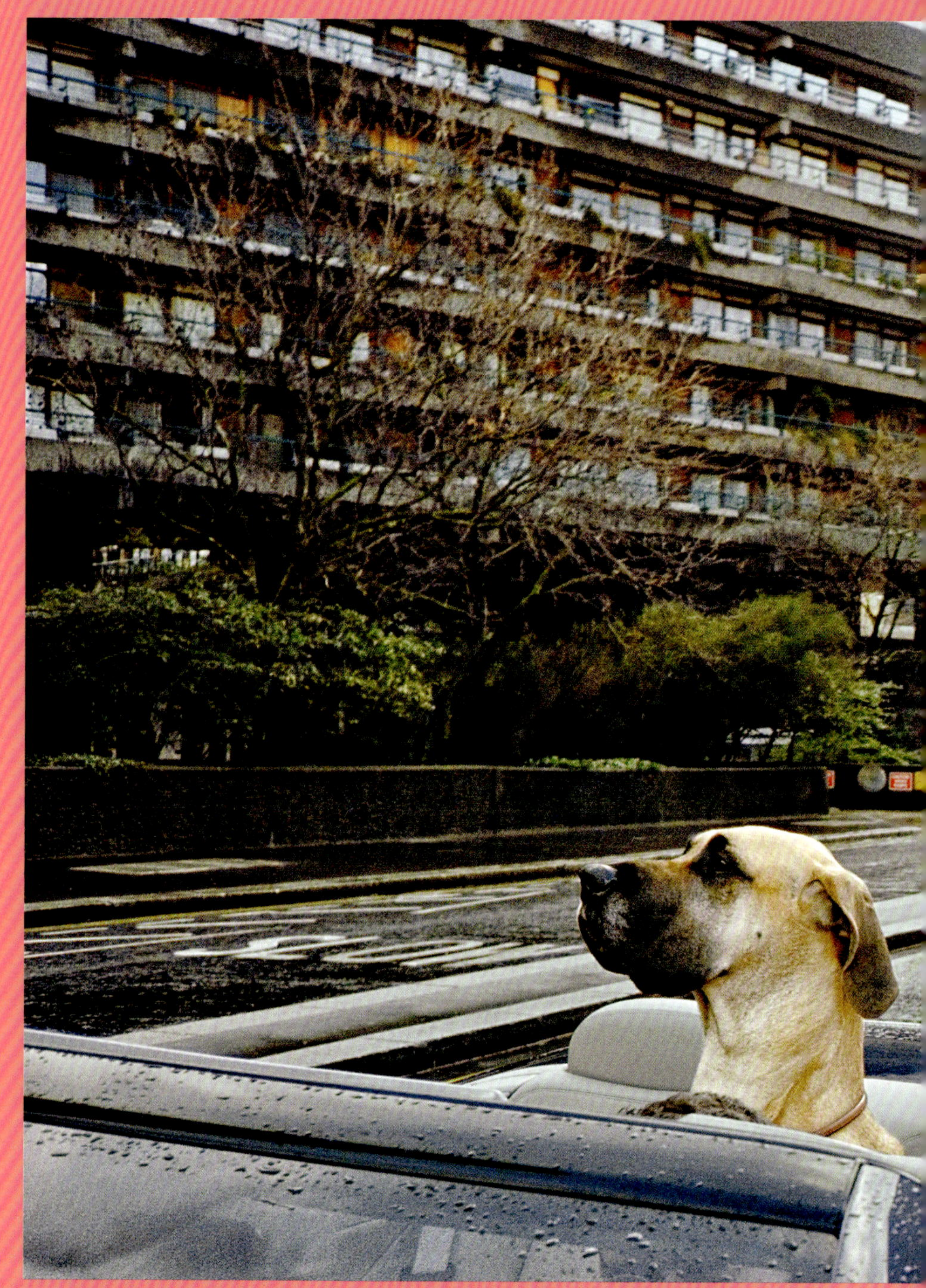

Aldersgate Street, London, 2006

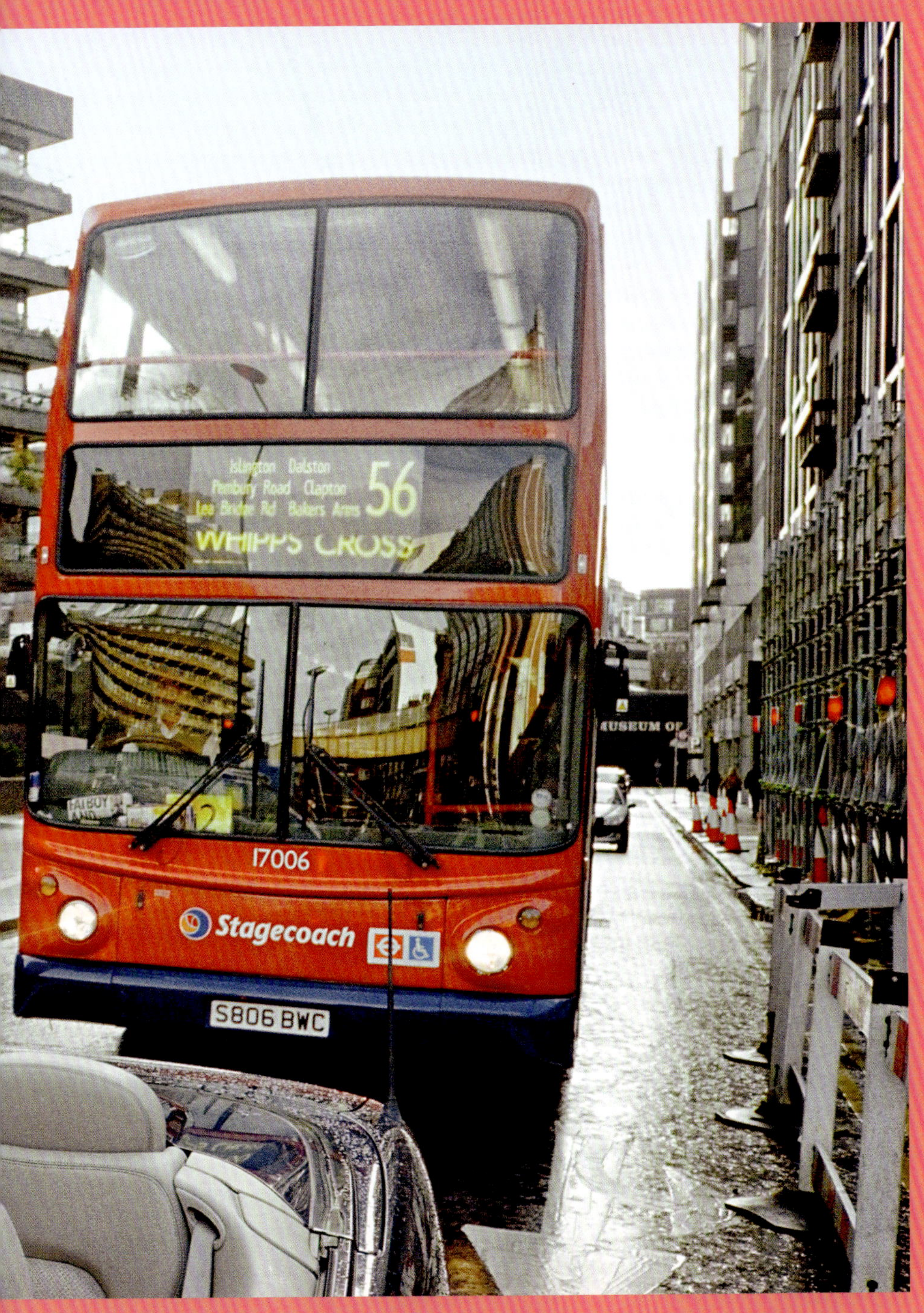

Islington Dalston
Pembury Road Clapton 56
Lea Bridge Rd Bakers Arms
WHIPPS CROSS
17006
Stagecoach
S806 BWC
MUSEUM OF

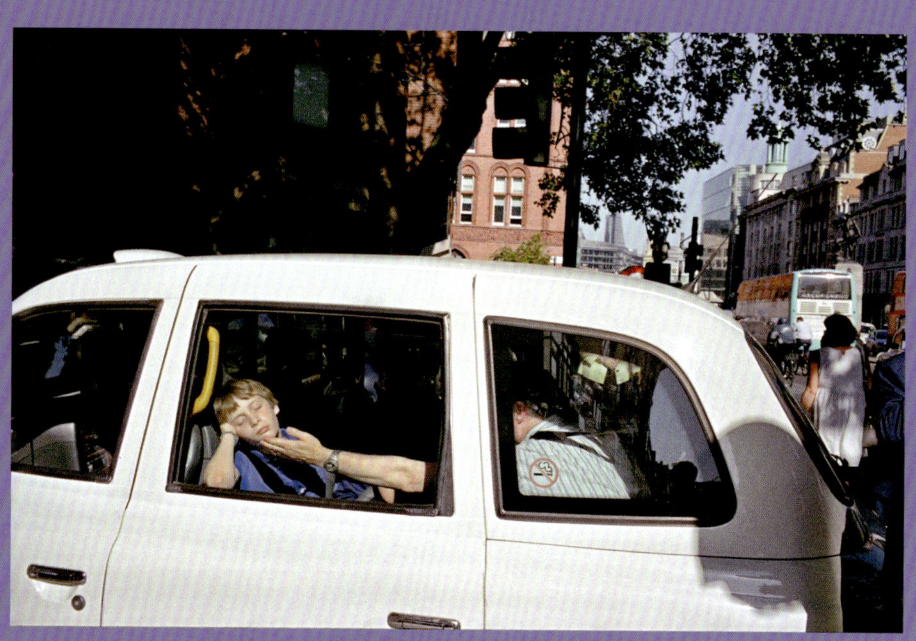

Theobald's Road, London, 2014

Chapter 4

BE CALM

Think fast, move slow

When you're on the street, you never quite know what
you're going to be faced with. You have to be able to change
your approach in relation to what comes at you.
Don't rush in – think about your body language and keep calm.

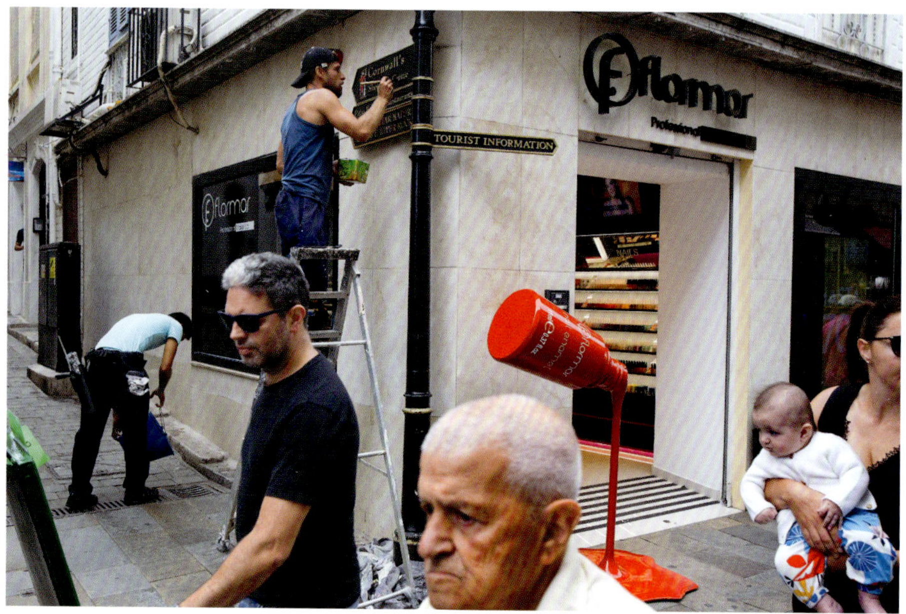

Gibraltar, 2017

When I 'discovered' photography, in my early twenties, I was excruciatingly keen. I still am, but at the beginning I was doing it every single day, for eight hours, for years. My dad, who liked to take pictures, had given me two books – one on Robert Frank, the other on Henri Cartier-Bresson. If Cartier-Bresson is single-handedly The Beatles of photography, Frank is The Rolling Stones.

I was working in a call centre at the time and my job was to placate angry people. I'd have the books on my lap and look through them every so often because the photographs of those great masters had the ability to whisk me away from it all. I was falling deeply, madly, head-over-heels in love with photography. From that point on, I knew I had to embark on a life dedicated to it.

Over the years, I've learned to blend into and move through crowds, which allows me to keep shooting relatively unnoticed. I don't have to get into talking to people, and, in the nicest possible way, I don't really want to talk to people because I'm busy being in my own head, making the pictures I want to make. That said, if someone catches me taking

'Street photography is not about rules... Don't let people tell you what to do. Do what feels right for you and your voice will come through.'

a picture, I'm more than happy to stop and explain why I took the photograph or ask if I can carry on shooting.

It's important to say that street photography is not about rules, and this is definitely not a rulebook – there are no rules but your rules. People create rules all the time when photographing: you can't speak to anyone, you have to shoot 35mm, you can't take the shot from the hip, you shouldn't use long lenses, you mustn't use flash or black and white. Don't let people tell you what to do. Do whatever feels right for you and your voice will come through. You don't want to be moulded by other people's thoughts or preconceptions of who you should be, or what you should be doing. It's important to find your own visual language.

I've tried many approaches. I've walked around people and deliberately got in people's way. I went through a phase of gently bumping into people to see what their reaction would be. No prizes for guessing how everyone responded. That was a while back and it was a short-lived experiment. One of the things I come back to time and again is the notion, somewhat perversely, of slowing down physically – not rushing in, but thinking fast. The cogs are whirring inside but outside I'm the epitome of calm. People spot you a mile off if you rush in.

Body language is also very important. I tend to bend my knees a lot, almost in a bowing gesture, and keep my elbows in (there's nothing worse than a photographer flapping their elbows around). A humble stance is more subtle. I also tend to wear muted colours – I don't want to stand out or catch people's attention. When it comes to the 'leaping into people's faces with a hard flash' genre of photography, I'll leave that to Bruce Gilden or Mark Cohen. Gilden stamped his authority on that and I wouldn't do it myself. That's not to say you can't get close to your subjects, and I do; I just

'You don't want to be moulded by other people's thoughts or pre-conceptions of who you should be... find your own visual language.'

prefer to do it in a way that is less confrontational. One of the best experiences for me, when shooting on the street, is being centimetres from someone's face for a few seconds and taking a picture without the person noticing I was there. In this situation, you're 'living' with them for a moment, making a record of the time you spent with them. There is nothing quite like it.

TRY THIS

When shooting in a town or city, make for the widest pavements you can because they allow more room to move, pivot and dodge. As you do, pay attention to how you're moving and how it affects the pictures you're making.

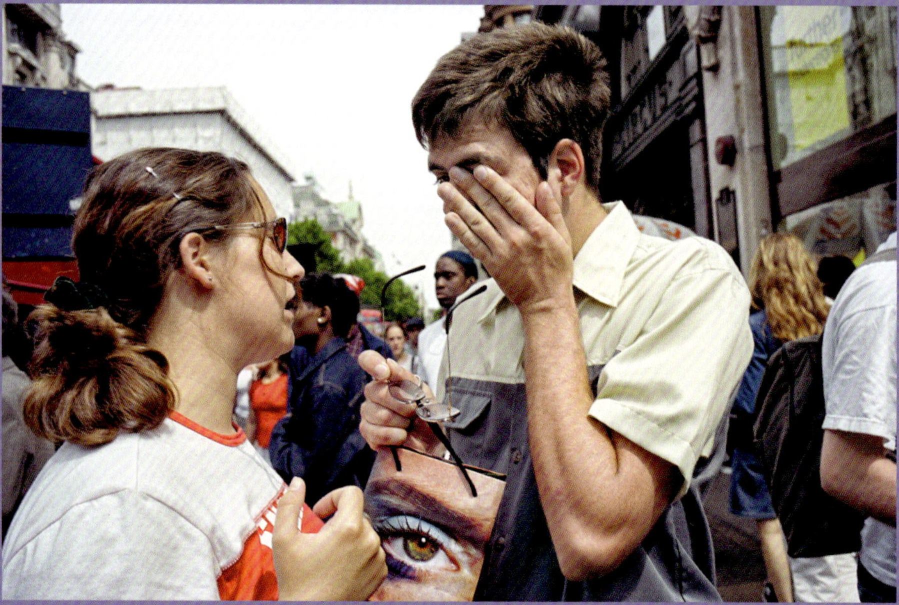

Oxford Circus, London, 2009

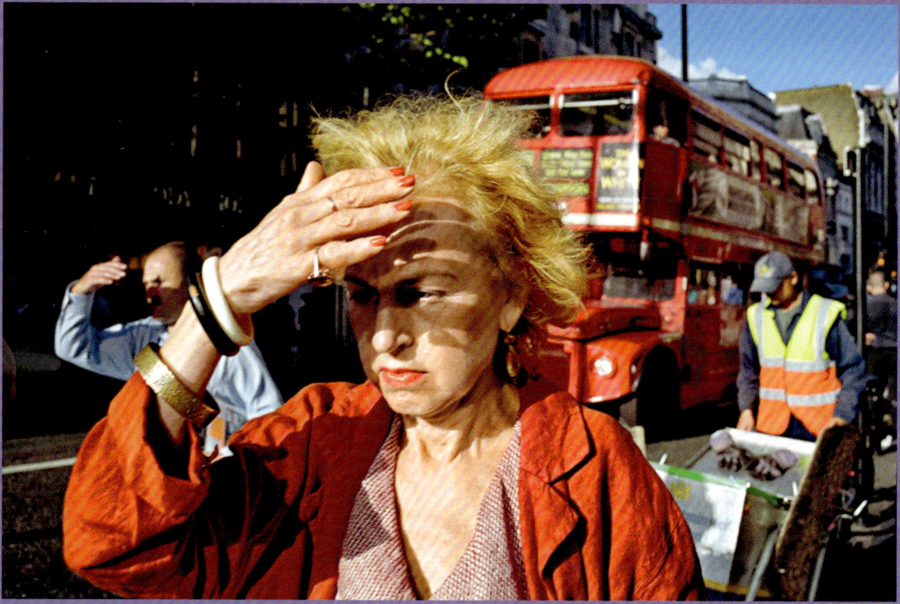

Oxford Street, London, 2004

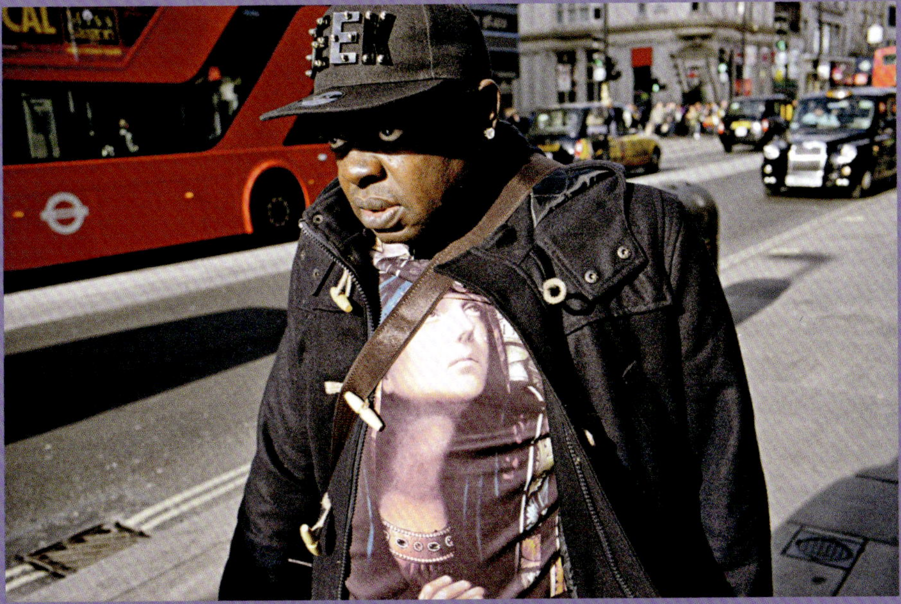

Oxford Street, London, 2014

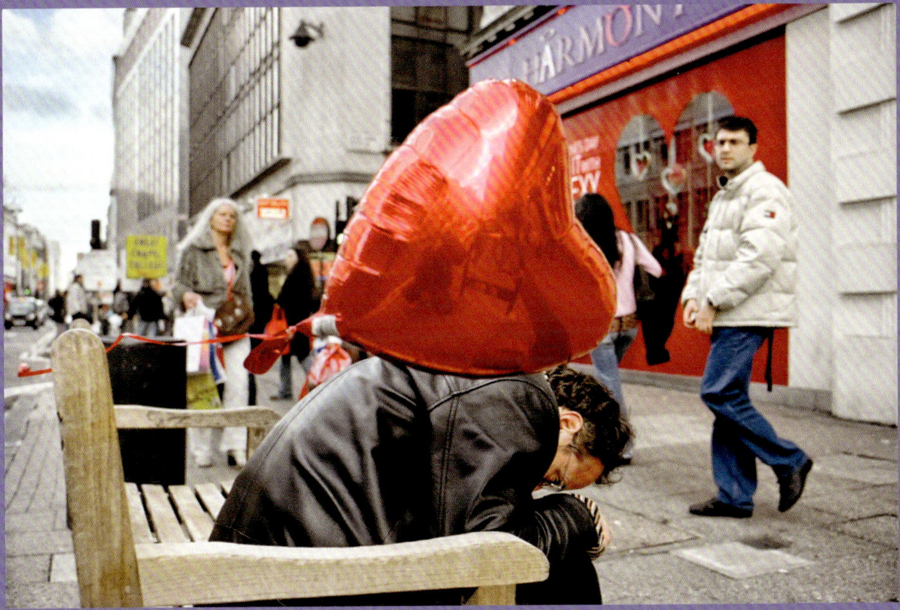

Oxford Street, London, 2008

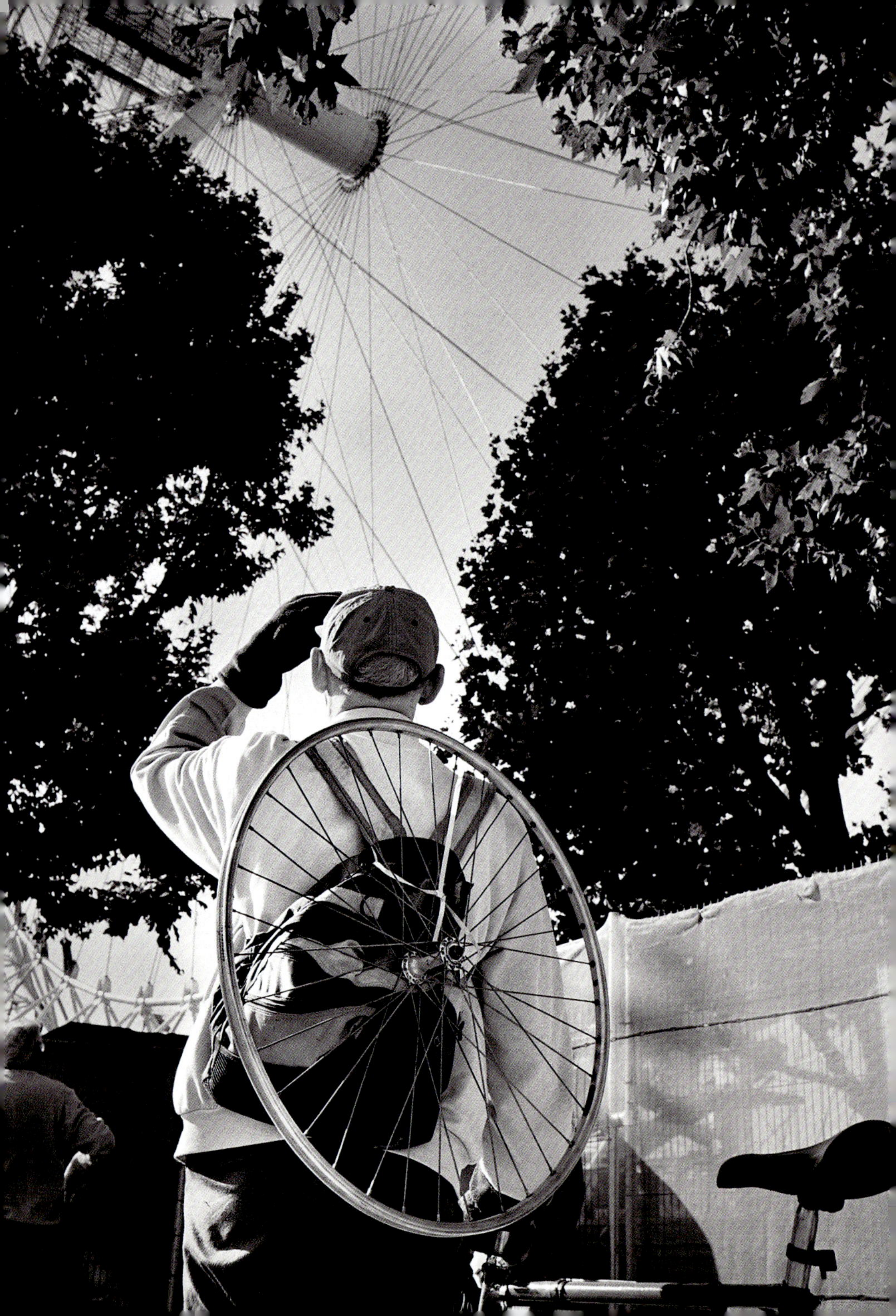

Chapter 5

IF AT FIRST YOU DON'T SUCCEED...

Practise, practise, practise

Street photography is the result of hard work rather than luck. You have to commit, spend hours on the street, and learn the art of saying 'yes' as opposed to saying 'no' if you want to succeed.

Never does that old maxim 'The harder I practise, the luckier I get' ring truer than with street photography. You have to put in the hours, pound the pavements, adopt a kind of 'in it to win it' mentality if you want to get anywhere.

The wheel photograph on page 28 is a good example of getting out what you put in. It was the end of 1999 and the London Eye was going up. I'd been photographing for about three years but was still inexperienced. I'd been on a workshop with Magnum photographer Leonard Freed and felt inspired. I went across the river on a Friday and photographed the workers as they were putting up the wheel, but nothing with any picture-making potential was happening. I went again on the Saturday and there were lots of tourists, but I didn't get much in the way of pictures. On the Sunday, around one or two o'clock in the afternoon, a guy with a wheel strapped to his back turned up, looked at the London Eye for a while, then got back on his bike and rode off. I was all fingers and thumbs. I realized this was a good moment, but I was so nervous. I ended up with 20 frames, most of them blurred, just one usable. It was the first time I felt I could truly call myself a photographer and the first photograph I considered to be a 'keeper'.

'Never does that old maxim "The harder I practise, the luckier I get" ring truer than with street photography.'

Pictures, especially the really good ones, don't come around very often. In a good year I might come away with ten 'keepers' – ones that are special. They're difficult to come by, but if you're out there trying, you are far more likely to get lucky.

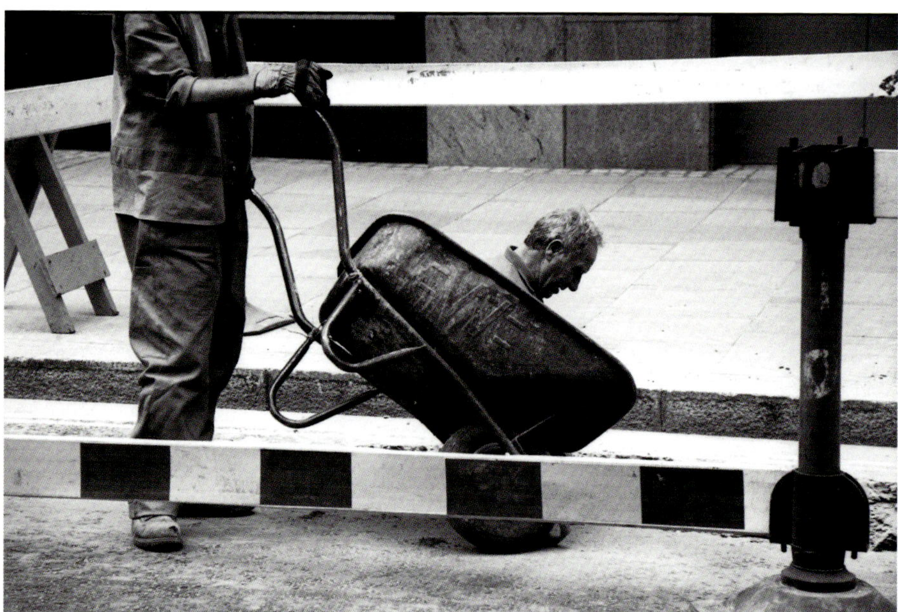

Page 28 Jubilee Gardens, London, 1999   Above Silk Street, London, 2002

If you think you can roll out of the door with a camera you haven't used in seven weeks, it's not going to happen. One of the key things is to give it time – not negative time but enjoyable, 'walking out in the fresh air' time. It's an investment – the more you put into it, the more it will pay off.

In *Outliers: The Story of Success* (2008), author and journalist Malcolm Gladwell famously presented the '10,000 Hour Rule', the basic premise of which is that after 10,000 hours of 'deliberate practice' you're going to be reasonably good at whatever it is you're doing. Although Gladwell's theory has been challenged and pored over, it's difficult not to agree with its basic sentiment.

Ultimately, it's about overcoming fear: the fear of not being good at something but also the fear of what might happen to us if we take the picture – what might that person do? What might they think or say? We all care what other people think, or rather, we are fearful that others might think badly of us. It's more about how much *we* care about how much *they* care, which they don't. Getting past that, I think, is important.

At the beginning of my workshops I get the participants to do exercises – literally physical exercises to wake everyone up. I ask them to do all the photo manoeuvres *we should never do*, such as the 'tourist squat' – feet apart, knees bent – and 'the lunge', a very anatomically correct camera-holding lurch. I also get them to exercise their right finger – up and down, up and down. It breaks the ice and encourages people to be less self-conscious and do silly things in a public place.

Humour and making things fun are important. They're about not taking yourself too seriously or getting hung up on trying to take the perfect picture, because thinking like that can be debilitating. Far better to let situations open up and give them a chance to become good enough, because you never know when something will come good.

The photograph on page 32 looks like a lucky shot, but I'd been following the man for a while. He had been taking part in a naked protest at Trafalgar Square. I followed him to the London Underground, photographing him from behind. Everything came together in this picture – the man, the text, the arrows and the CCTV camera – but there is a whole roll of other pictures I'd taken; with every shot I was hoping the next would be better.

The picture on page 33 of a woman asleep on a train underneath a poster is almost pre-visualized. The content is real but it's an idea that came to fruition through perseverance, and also obsession. I'd noticed this advert and thought it would be great to get someone asleep under it. It took two weeks of travelling on the Underground, and of looking and photographing, to get this shot.

TRY THIS

Sunglasses immediately cut off eye contact, which is essential to gaining trust. Headphones stop you from hearing. Smiling makes you look friendly. Choose one of the above and give it a go.

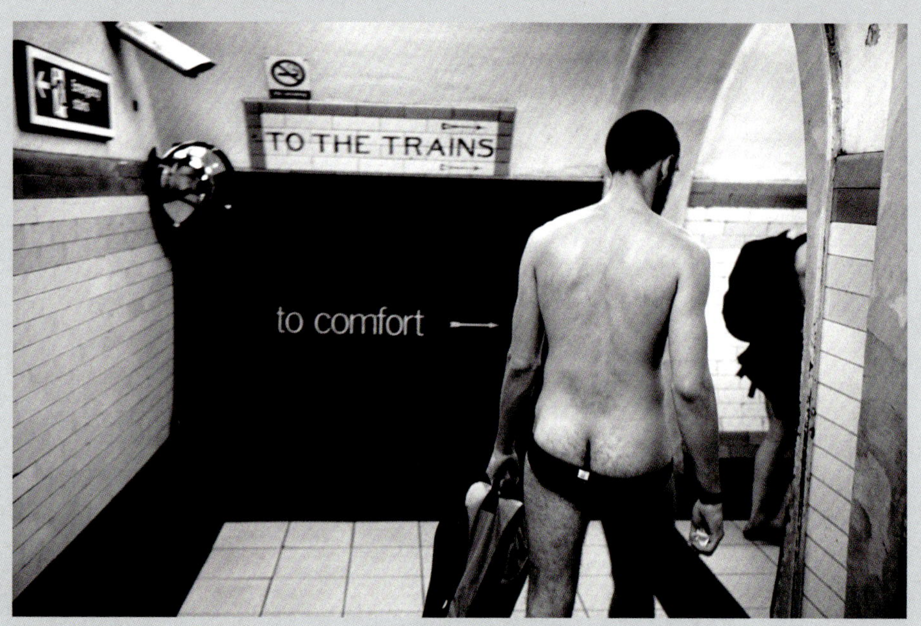

Covent Garden Underground station, London, 2001

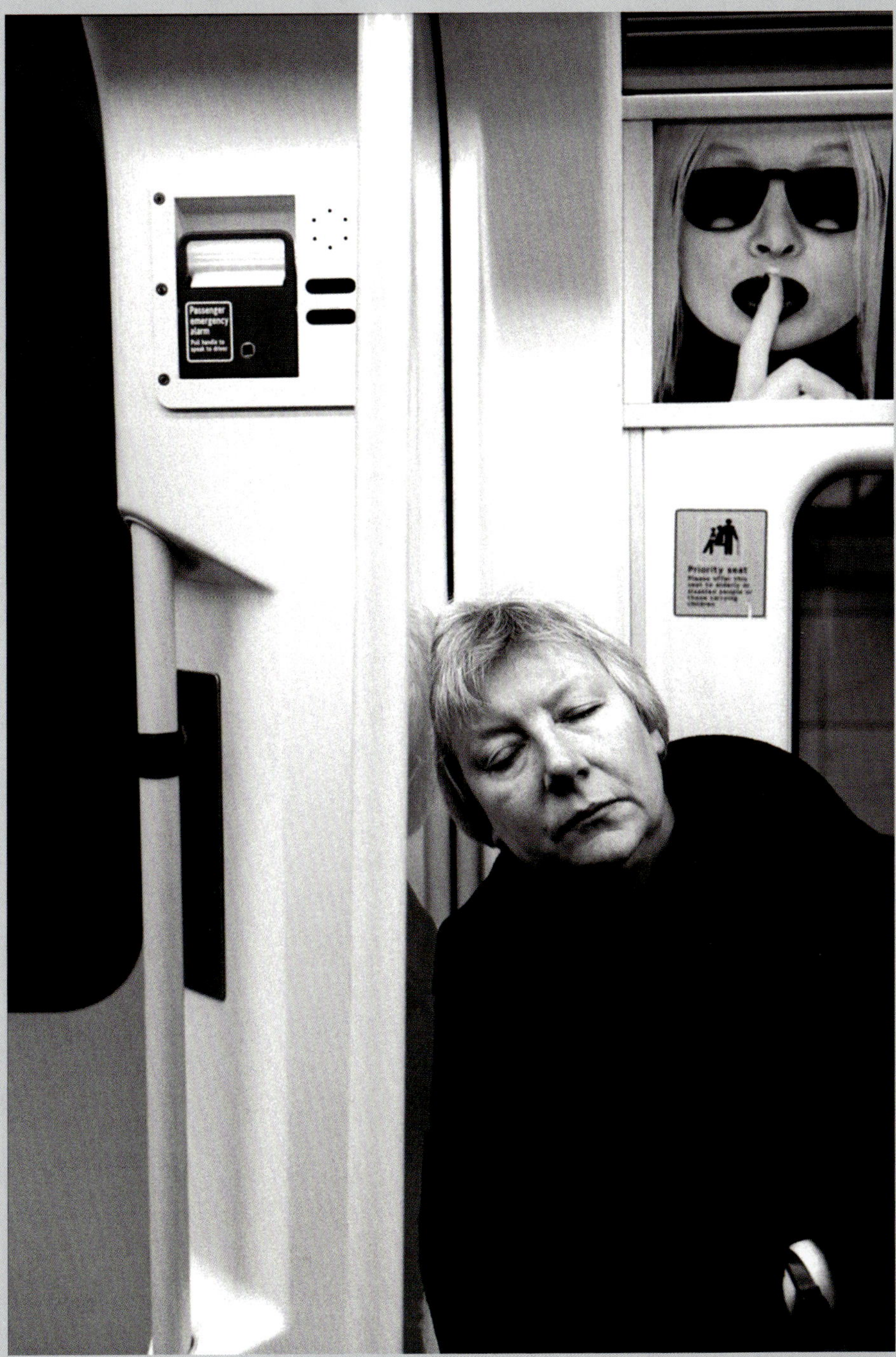

Bank Underground station, London, 2000

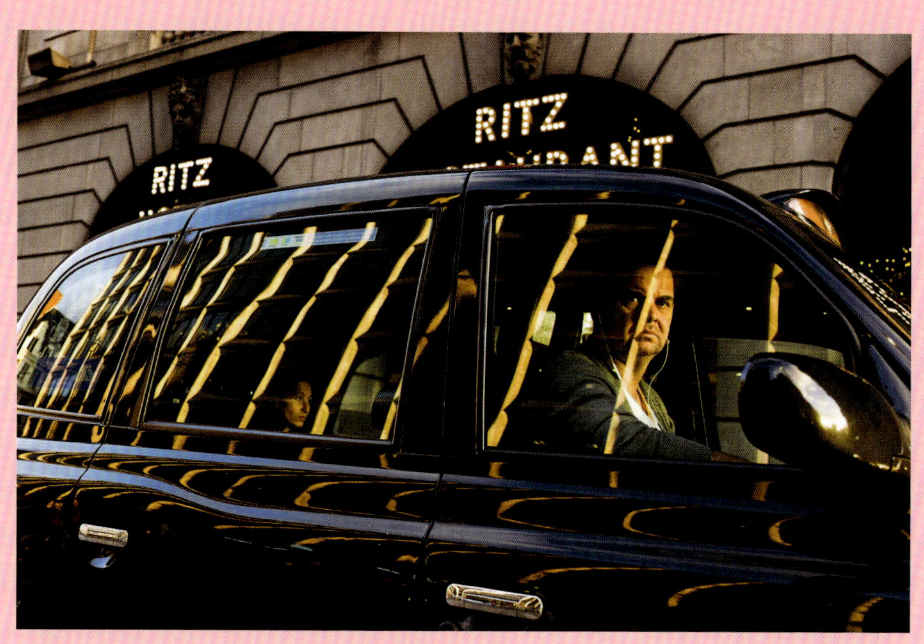

Piccadilly, London, 2018

Chapter 6

KEEP IT SIMPLE

Don't be blinded by technology

Don't get bogged down by the technical stuff. It's good to know the basics, but don't let them get in the way when you spot something interesting on the street. If you're more focused on your camera than the scene itself, you might just lose the shot.

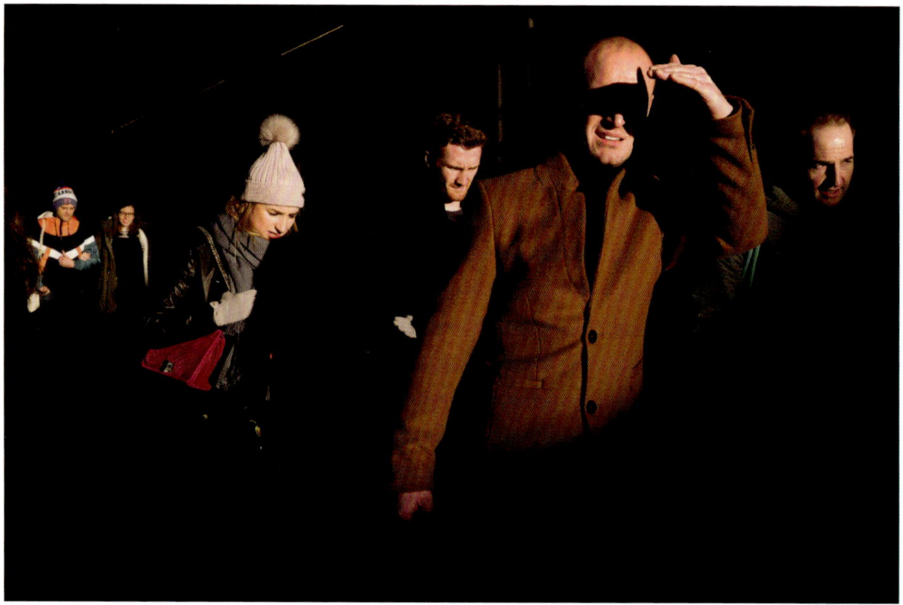

Piccadilly, London, 2018

want to make one thing absolutely clear: this isn't a technique-focused book. There are plenty of books out there already that cover the techie stuff, some brilliantly. Besides, knowing the intricate ins and outs of your camera is all very well until you're in the thick of it, on the street with people coming at you from every direction. You don't want to be fussing over your camera settings as an opportunity presents itself, or a potential subject approaches and then passes you by.

That said, in order to set out with confidence and make the pictures you want to make, you should familiarize yourself with your camera's settings and know just enough so that you're not fumbling around with the dial when you're on the street. At the very least, play around with the shutter speed and see how changing it affects your pictures in different conditions.

I have a really simple approach… let's not call it a rule. Most of the things I shoot

'You don't want to be fussing over your camera settings as an opportunity presents itself, or a potential subject approaches and then passes you by.'

during the day are taken at 1/1000 sec. The reason 1/1000 sec is important is that if you bring a camera up to your eye really quickly because you've seen something, nine times out of ten the shot will be sharp as long as you've got the focus right, because 1/1000 sec is a fast shutter speed.

It all boils down to whether conditions are sunny or overcast. On an overcast day in the UK you're probably looking at 1/1000 sec at f/4, shooting with ISO 800. And that means the main subject will be sharp. On a sunny day, 1/1000 sec

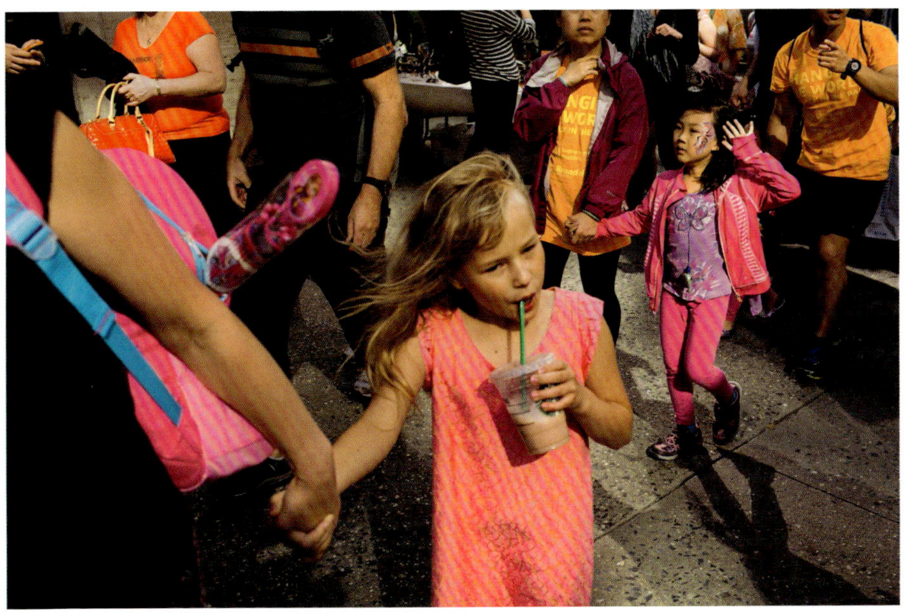

Fifth Avenue, New York, 2015

at f/11, or even f/16 means that everything's going to be sharp all the way through. So I just constantly have the camera set to 1/1000 sec and use whatever aperture is already selected. As a street photographer, I believe reaction comes first, so my first setting during the day is always the shutter speed.

At night time I work from a wide-open aperture on my camera because I want to let in as much light as possible in order to maintain a high shutter speed while shooting.

'When it comes to the technical stuff... pare it back... If you can shut down some of the variables, do so, because this will free you up to focus on what really matters.'

The best advice I can offer, then, when it comes to the technical stuff, is to pare it back. Don't make life harder for yourself than it needs to be. If you can shut down some of the variables, do so, because this will free you up to focus on what really matters: the seeing – seeing what's happening around you, reading situations and anticipating what's about to happen. In the words of the great Elliott Erwitt: 'All the technique in the world doesn't compensate for the inability to notice.'

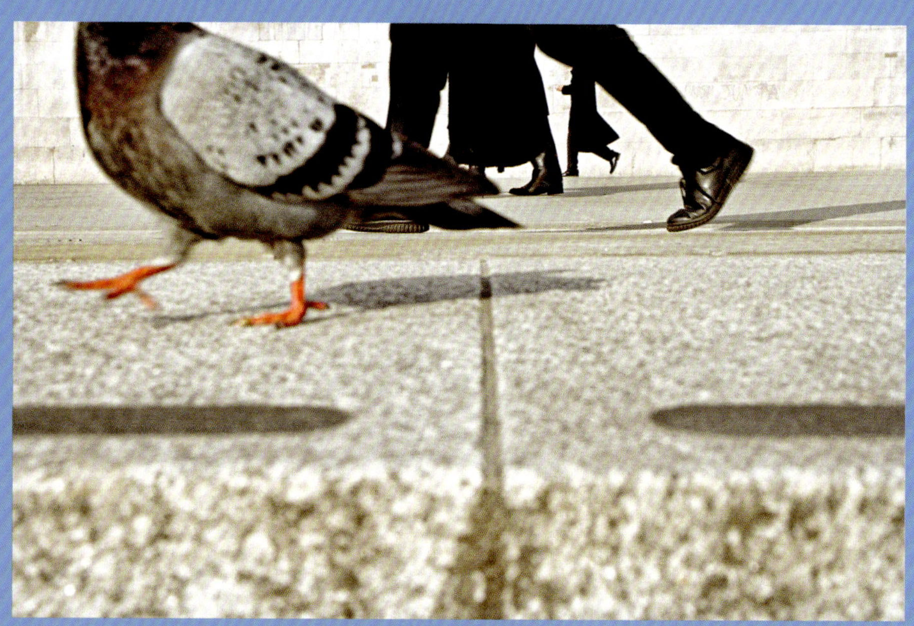

Trafalgar Square, London, 2004

SEE WITH A CHILD'S EYES

Keep your eyes peeled and your ears to the ground

Be open to everything when you're out shooting. If your eye is 'on', the pictures will come and the little curiosities that life throws up will suddenly appear everywhere for the taking.

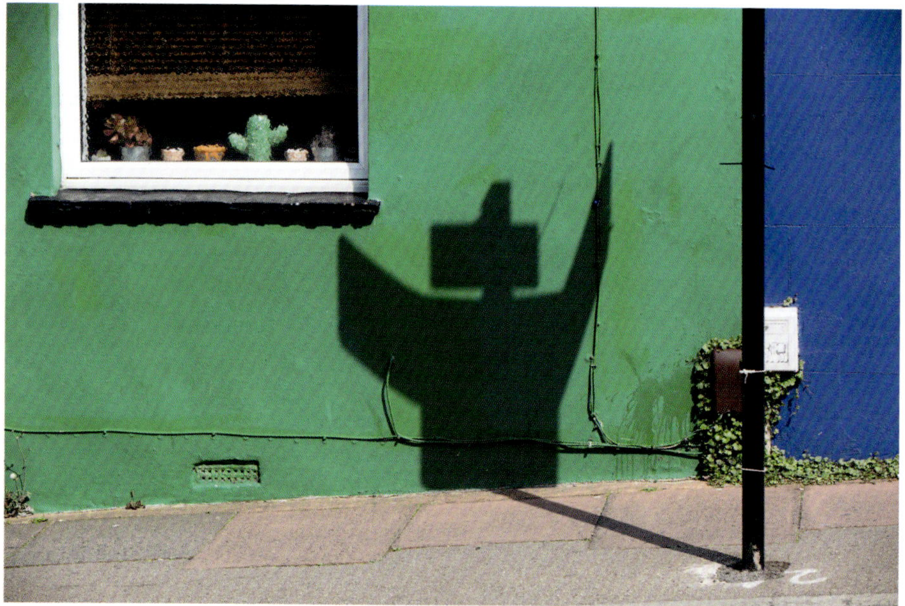

Brighton, 2018

f you've ever been out and about on foot with a young child, you'll know all too well that a five-minute journey can take much, much longer. Not just because of the tantrums, but rather the frequent stopping and starting as they point to things that have caught their eye. Young children, especially those who are learning to speak, will often point and name what they see, 'Dog! Bus! Ball!'

I'm not suggesting we all start to play the 'say what you see' game, but there is something in this childlike way of seeing the world, in allowing yourself to focus on whatever catches your attention in a given moment, and seeing from a new, uninhibited perspective. If you can learn to see innocently as a child sees – to notice bright colours, combinations of things, mini narratives, funny street furniture or happenings – you'll be on the road to developing a way of seeing that is essential to street photography.

The day I made the image of a marching pigeon (page 38), a photograph that has become one of my best known, was in truth a slightly boring day. I had gone out but was feeling a little bit as though I was twiddling my thumbs. I ended up at Trafalgar Square and sat down on the steps opposite The National Gallery. I started looking through my camera

'If you can learn to see... as a child sees... you'll be on the road to developing a way of seeing that is essential to street photography.'

at street level and began noticing all these feet that were going backwards and forwards, and making interesting shapes. This is the kind of thing that

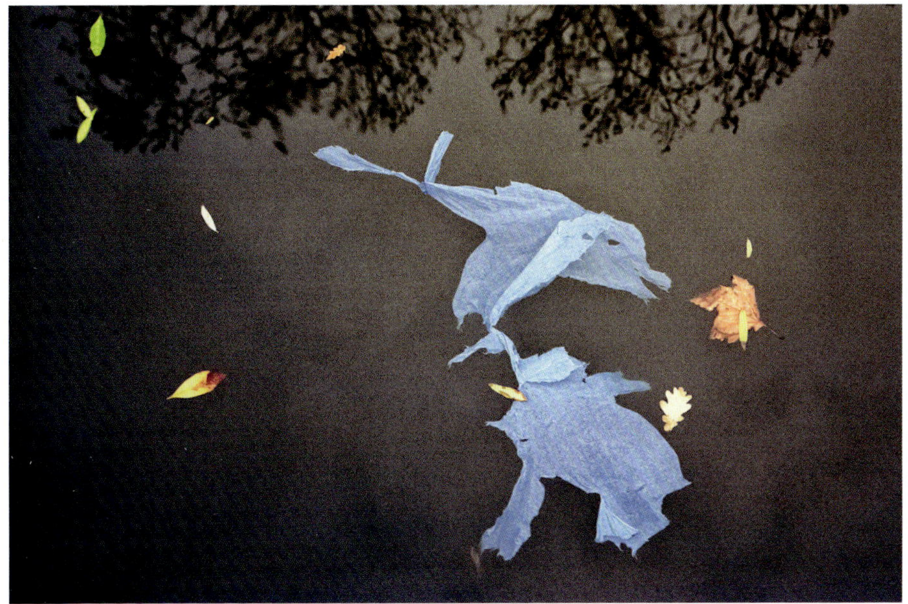

Regent's Canal, London, 2010

keeps me occupied for ages, and I must have spent about half an hour photographing legs going past. I was huddled up in a ball and probably had my bottom in the air as I was looking through the viewfinder. The pigeons started walking really close to me. One particularly cocky pigeon walked up and down three or four times – it was almost as though it was promenading. I made two or three pictures, one of which felt really right.

When I looked at the picture on the contact sheet it was a lovely surprise. Everything had come together. The mirroring of the pigeon's tail and the tail of the coat, the pigeon's feet going forward, the guy inside the white triangle with his feet echoing the pigeon's – everything was pretty much perfect. So I was very lucky. That word again!

The pigeon shot was in one sense a happy accident, but it came about because I had put myself in a position where I was literally looking from a different point of view. The picture on pages 44–45 is another example. I was walking through Hyde Park in London and came across the scene of a child holding a balloon, which had a real *Alice in Wonderland* quality to it. As I started taking pictures, the man with the dog began pointing at the ground, trying to make the dog sit. Nobody saw me photographing. I felt completely invisible. I liked that feeling of being able to capture the scene and then leave it without influencing it in any way.

Street photography gives you a unique pass to participate in a situation without others necessarily knowing you are there. This I believe is one of the reasons we keep coming back to it: the invisible participation, followed by the visible proof that you were there and saw or felt something.

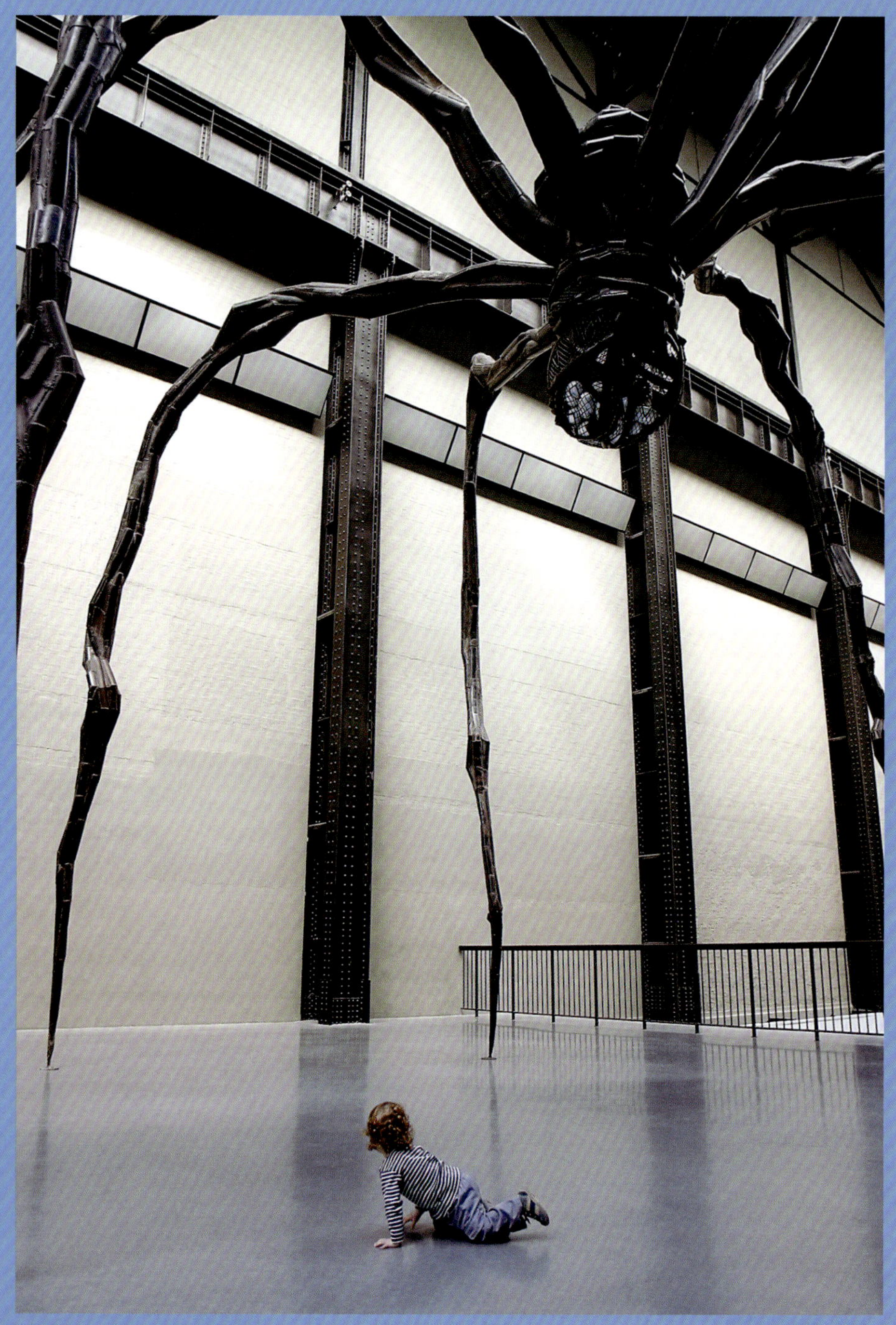

Tate Modern, London, 2002

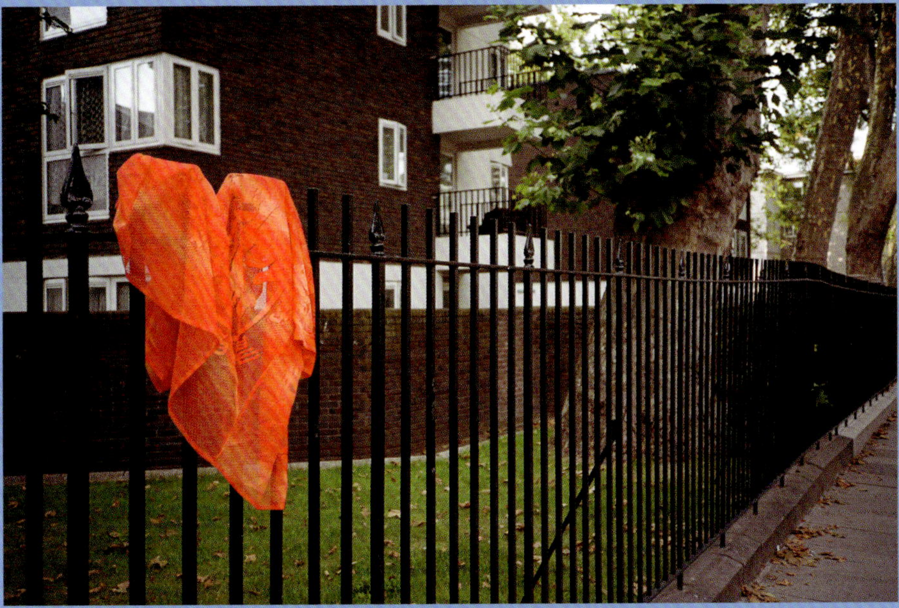

Guildford Street, London, 2007

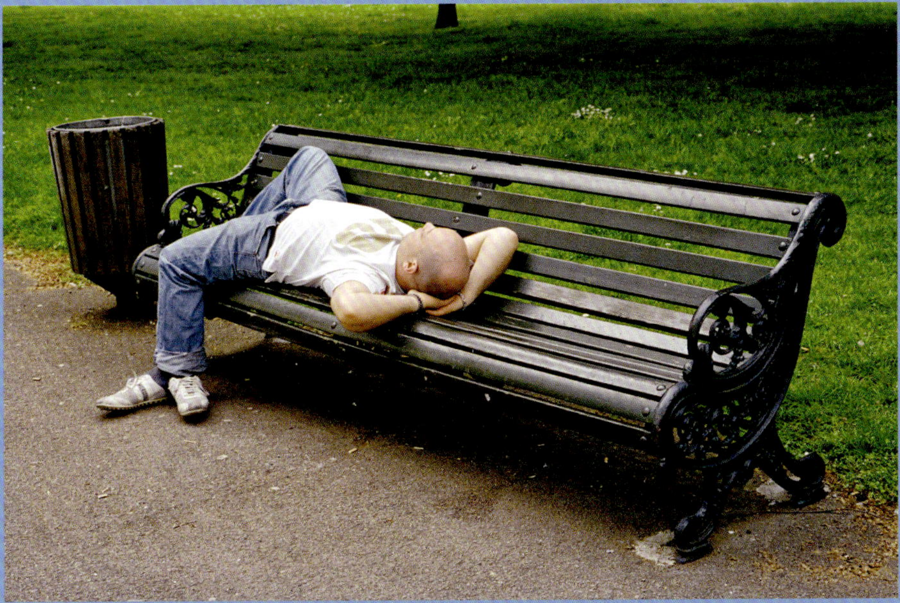

Hyde Park, London, 2009

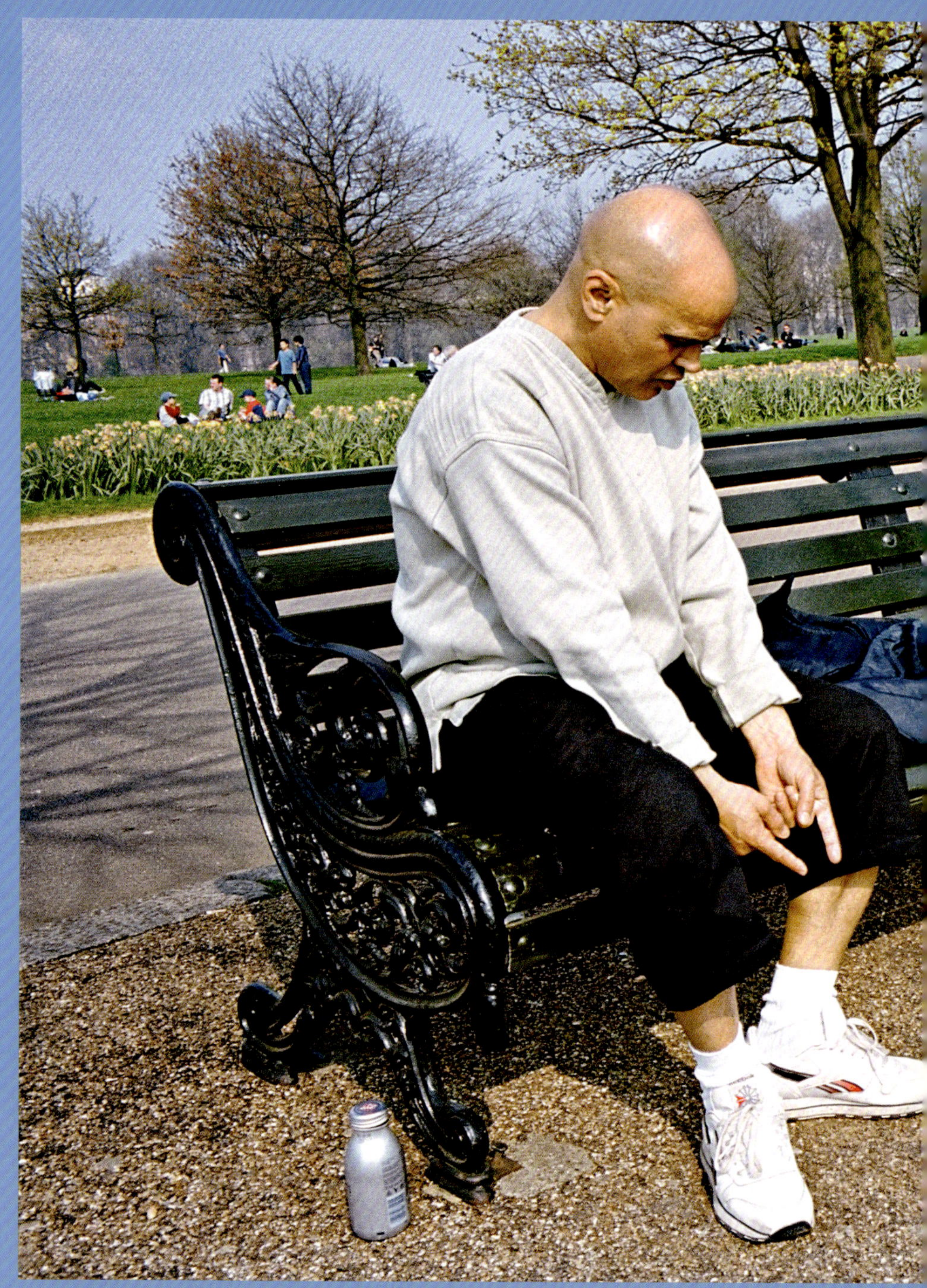

Hyde Park, London, 2008

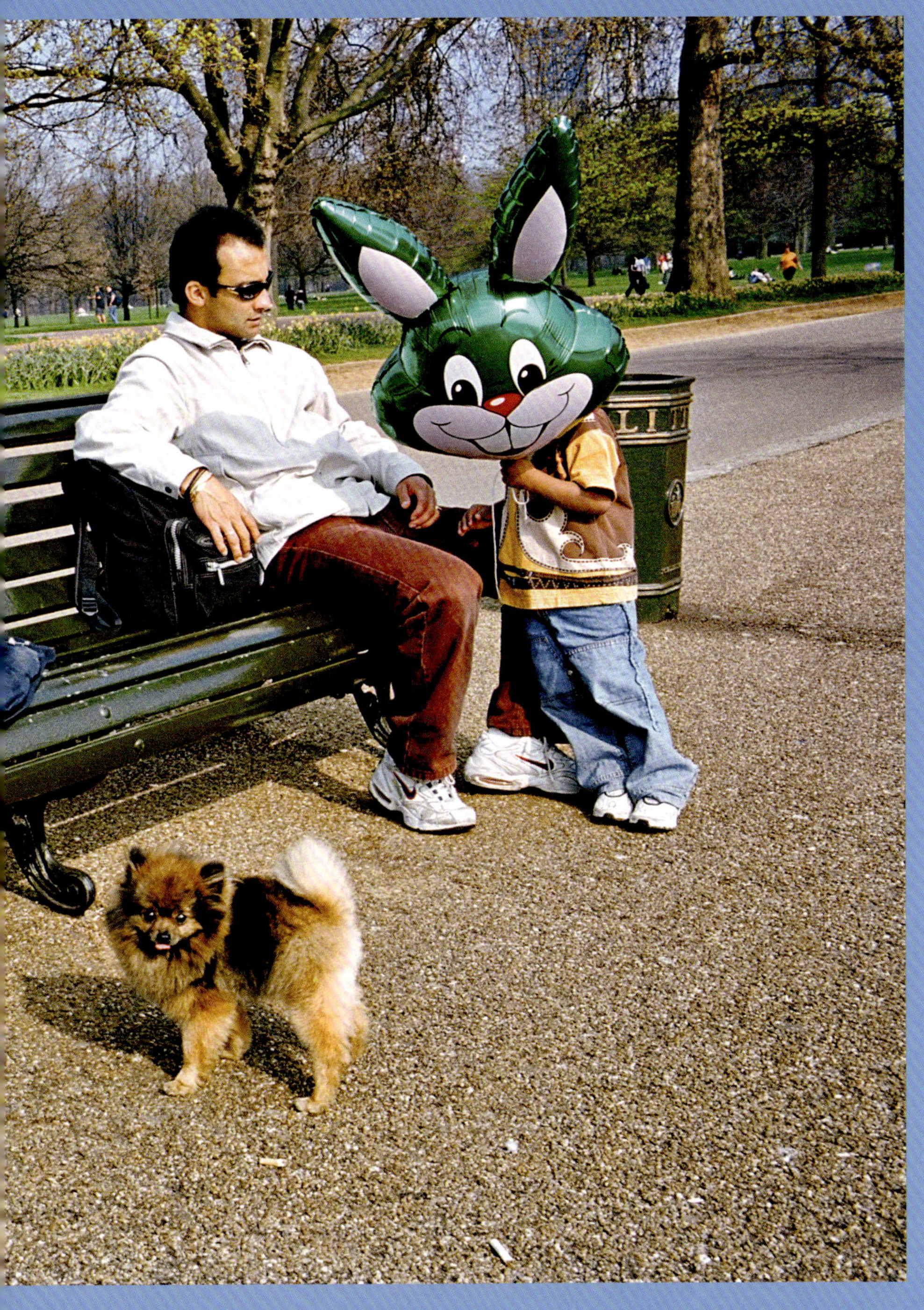

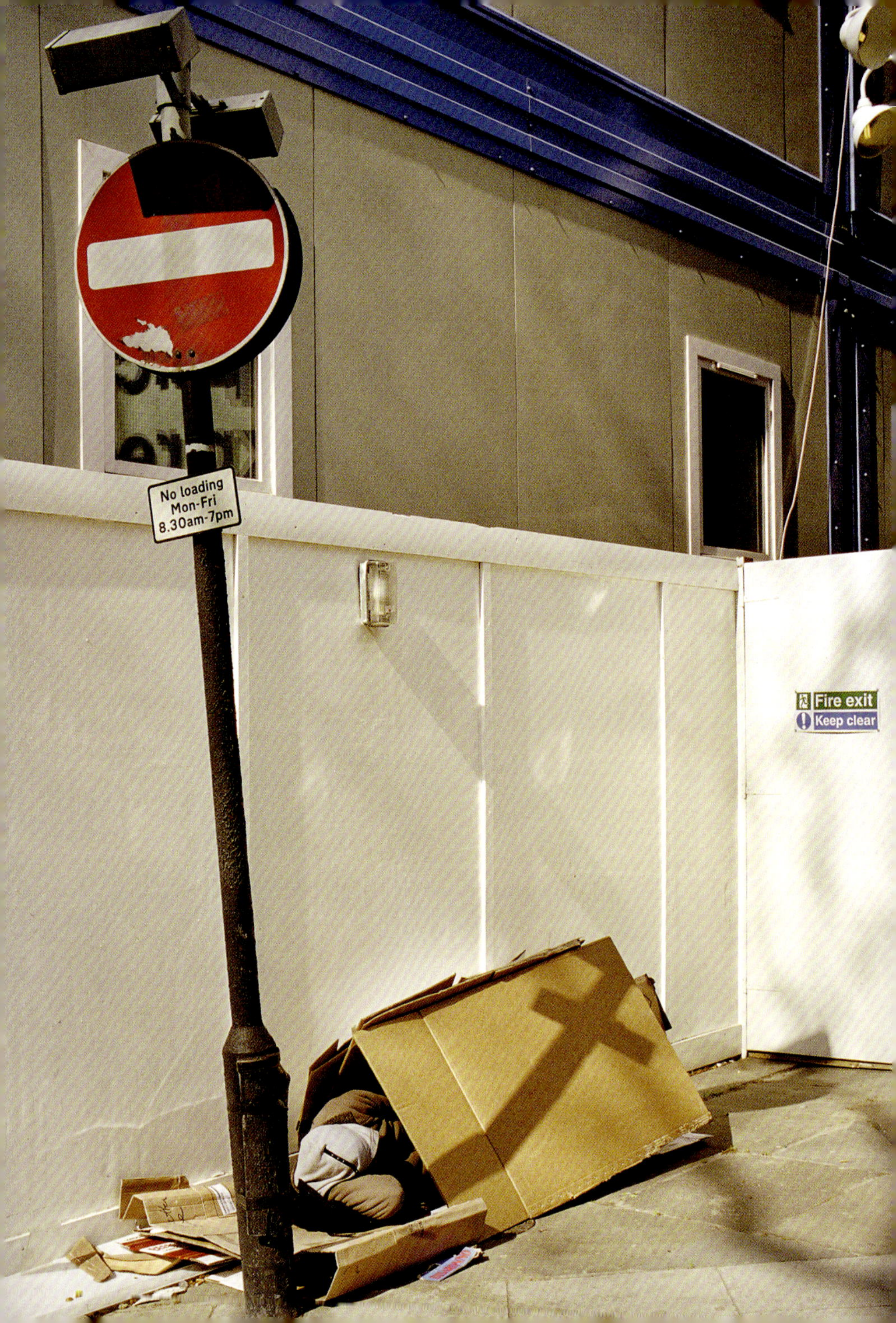
No loading
Mon-Fri
8.30am-7pm
Fire exit
Keep clear

Chapter 8

SHOOT FIRST, THINK LATER

If in doubt, press the shutter

Avoid the trauma of 'the one that got away' at all costs. If you don't even try, if you don't push yourself to give it a go, or stop to ask yourself whether the shot is worth the effort, you might just miss it.

We've all experienced moments of hesitation and doubt about whether we're able to capture the picture: 'Am I framing it right? I'm not sure I've got a good exposure.' We also ask ourselves whether we should in fact take the shot: 'What will happen if I press the shutter? Is it OK to make a picture?' These, I'll bet, are thoughts most street photographers have had at some point in their picture-making lives.

When you're out and you see something that you think is worth photographing, shoot first and think later about whether you're going to show the picture. Go with your gut instinct because if you don't even attempt the picture, you might regret not trying. On the other hand, if you've had a go – even if it doesn't come to anything – at least you tried.

You have to ask yourself what is the worst that could happen? OK, you might die, but how likely is that really? You might be punched, but again, how likely is that? Most people aren't in the busi-

'When you're out and you see something you think is worth photographing, shoot first and think later about whether you're going to show the picture.'

ness of punching. The worst that could happen is the person tells you to 'F**k off!', which isn't very nice, but it's not the end of the world. If you are shooting with good intentions these types of situations don't usually happen.

One of the first things you tend to be told at college or university, or on street-photography forums, is not to photograph homeless people. I totally disagree. I think you should photograph the homeless, I think you should photograph the disabled, I think you should photograph everyone and everything because they exist. If the scene is interesting enough, you should take it. But knowing whether or not it's an interesting scene is another matter.

One of the first things that will get

'If the scene is interesting enough, you should take it. But knowing whether or not it's an interesting scene is another matter.'

you into trouble is thinking that something is interesting but then wondering if it's worth the effort. Is it going to make a good picture? Is it *worth* making a picture? The more you think about what you're shooting and why, the better sense you'll get of what's worth photographing. It's about engaging a degree of emotional intelligence (and being aware of your intent, see chapter 9). As Elliott Erwitt claims, 'Quality has to do with intention.'

Take the picture on page 46 of a homeless person in a box. I saw the scene and thought, 'Should I photograph him? Is this OK?' Then I noticed the cross-shaped shadow falling on the box, potentially making it more than just a picture of a homeless man sleeping – it could allude to the crisis of homelessness and be interpreted as a comment on society, which tends to walk on by. Besides, I thought, you can't see the man's face. In the end, I couldn't let it go. It's become one of my favourite photographs.

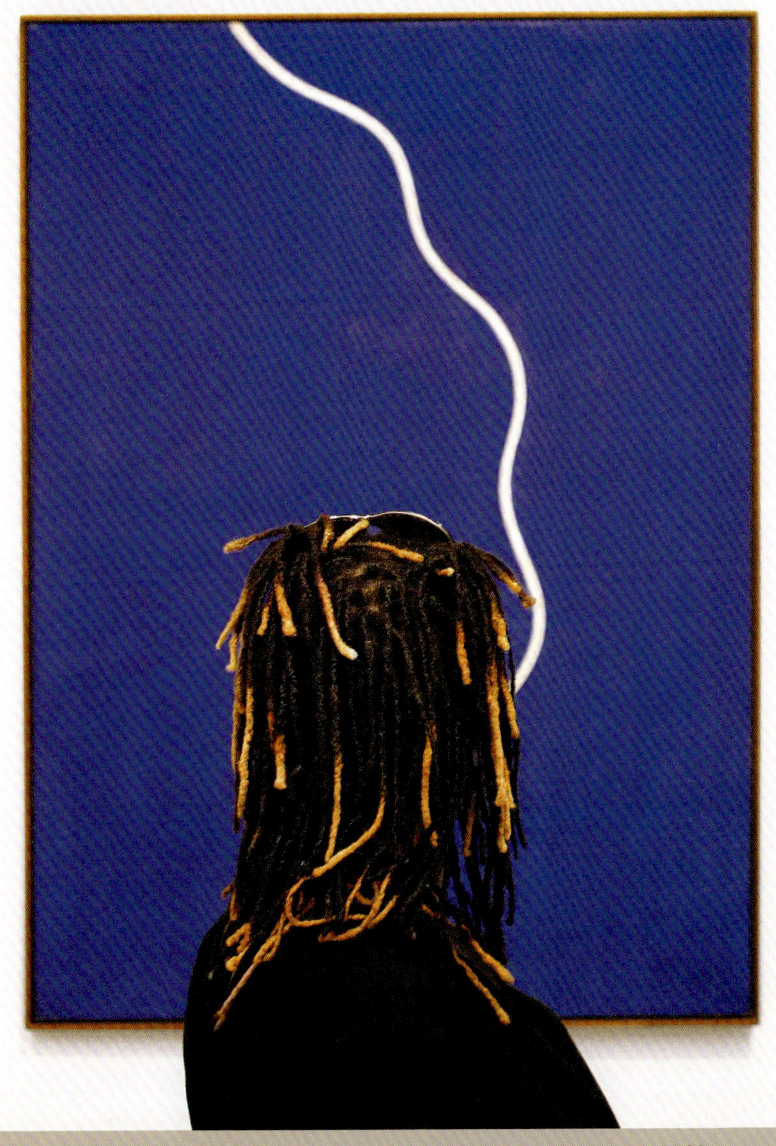

Page 46 Shaftesbury Avenue, London, 2010   **Above** Tate Modern, London, 2002

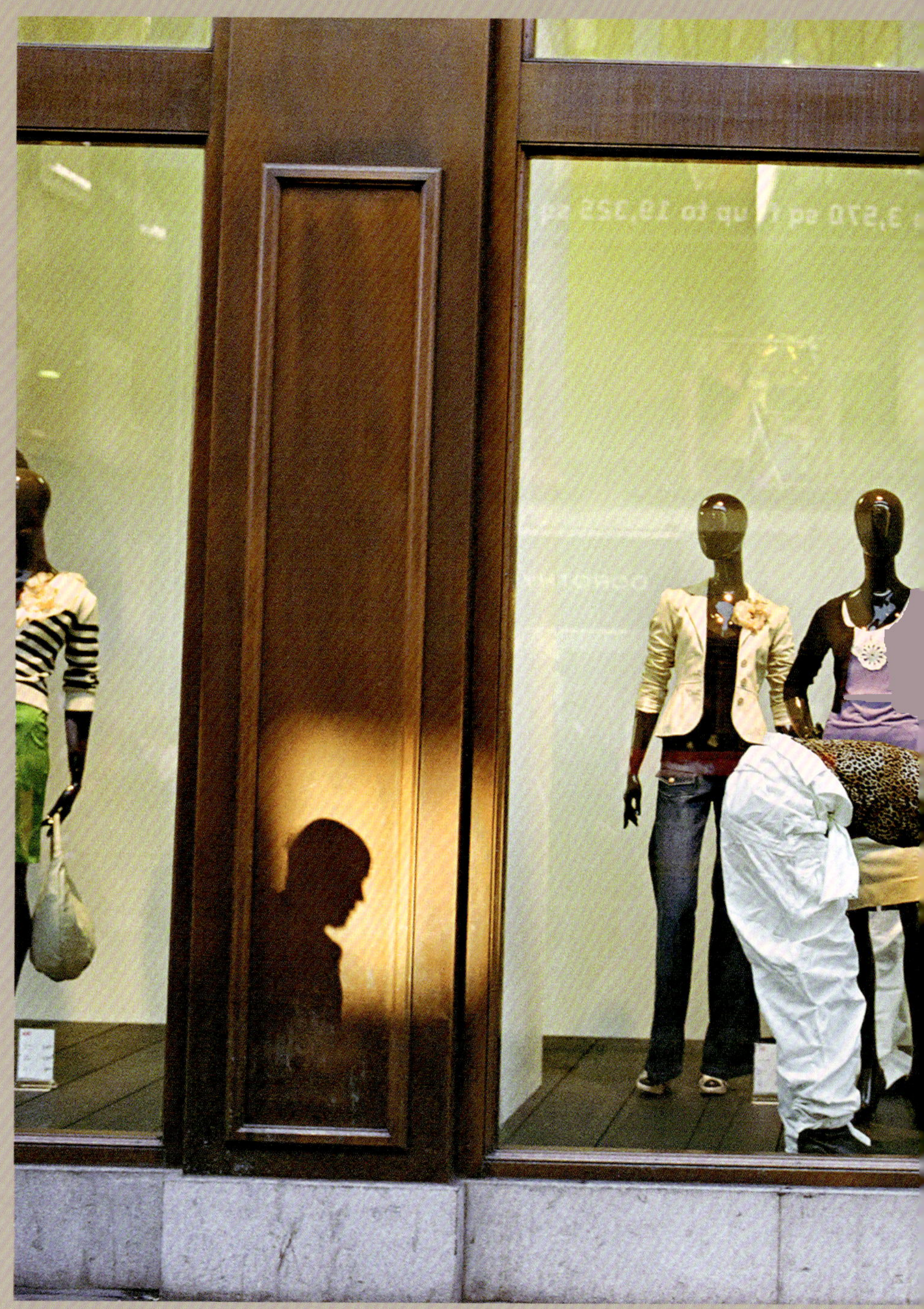

Oxford Street, London, 2009

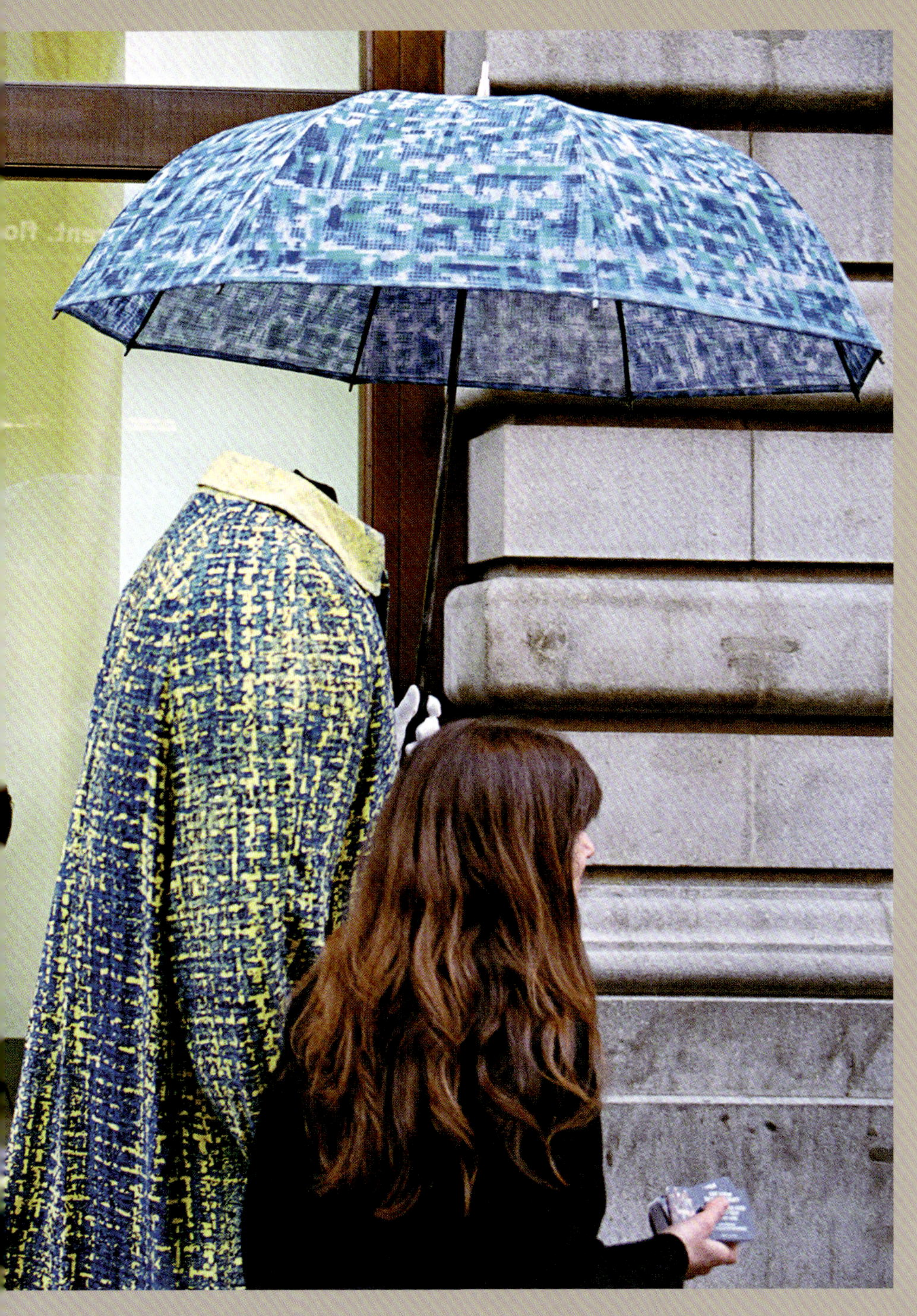

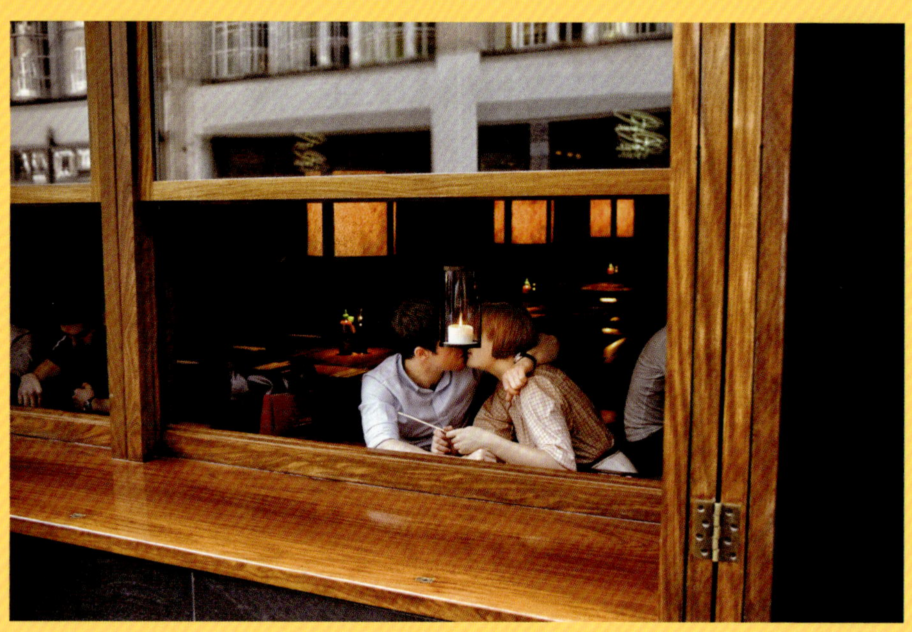

Wardour Street, London, 2010

Chapter 9

BE GOOD

Ethics on the street

Be thoughtful about how you are presenting your subject, and aware of when you might be invading someone's privacy. Approach the people you are photographing with sensitivity. Be open and honest.

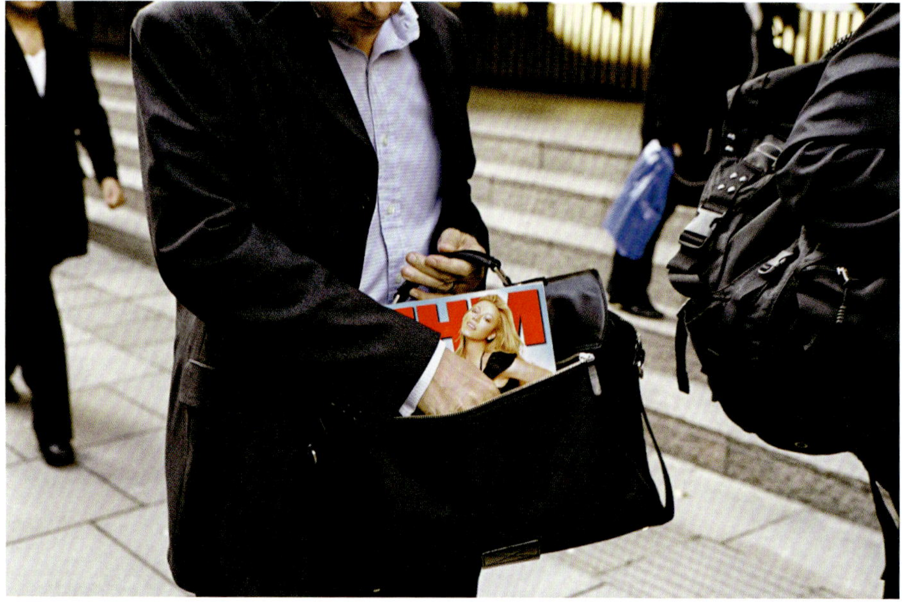

Liverpool Street, London, 2005

If ever there was a can of worms in street photography, it's ethics. Photographing in public is something of an ethical minefield because schools of thought on what is acceptable differ enormously from place to place, and from person to person, even though, in the UK at least, you legally have the right to photograph in a public place.

I'm fine with photographing children, though perhaps not naked ones running around on the beach – unless I've made sure it's OK with the parents. Animals don't have any rights as far as being photographed in public goes (although their owners might beg to differ).

A key thing to remember is that you're not allowed to photograph people from inside restaurants or shops, as these are classed as private property. What about photographing them from the street? This is something of a grey area. Technically, it's OK as long as you're in a public place, but

it's best to be discreet and quick. Having said that, every situation should be taken on its own merits. The only time I've had a run-in with someone was when I made the picture opposite of a man's legs and a dollar bill. The man who is reflected in the mirror came at me because he thought I was a health-and-safety inspector about to criticize him because the ladder wasn't being held.

As far as general ethics are concerned, I know I'm ethical and most of the things I photograph are generally taken in a good spirit. But you can get caught out. I was photographing an old lady once who was an interesting character. She was sitting down during some kind of parade or public event and a police officer came over and told me to stop taking pictures. I asked, 'What do you mean?' And he said, 'You should stop photographing up that woman's skirt.' I replied, 'I'm sorry officer, I'm not photographing up the woman's skirt, I'm simply photographing the woman.' Needless to say, the thought hadn't even crossed my mind but, in hindsight, maybe that is what it had looked like.

Be intelligent about what you're doing, and mindful about how it is coming across, however innocent you know it to be. Don't picture a subject in a way that you yourself wouldn't like to be pictured. If it's not in the subject's best interests, walk on.

At one workshop I gave, I kept telling the group to make sure their intentions were good. Nevertheless, one of the participants photographed two men fighting and they turned on him. It probably wasn't even a good picture anyway, and certainly not worth almost getting punched for.

If you encounter the 'Why are you taking my picture?' moment, one of the worst things you can say is, 'Because I have the right to.' It's a sure-fire way to piss people off. If you're honest about what interests you about them – their appearance or what they might be doing – they will usually be more open to having been photographed.

TRY THIS

If the person whose photo you are taking confronts you, be open and honest. Say, 'I really like such and such about you.' If your intentions are good, it will show. Liars often hesitate!

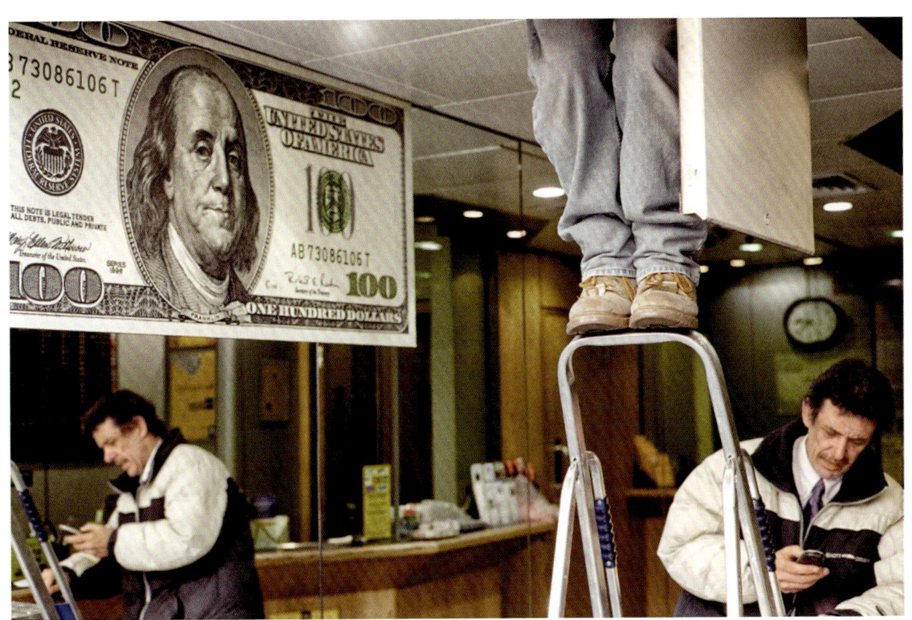

Oxford Street, London, 2004

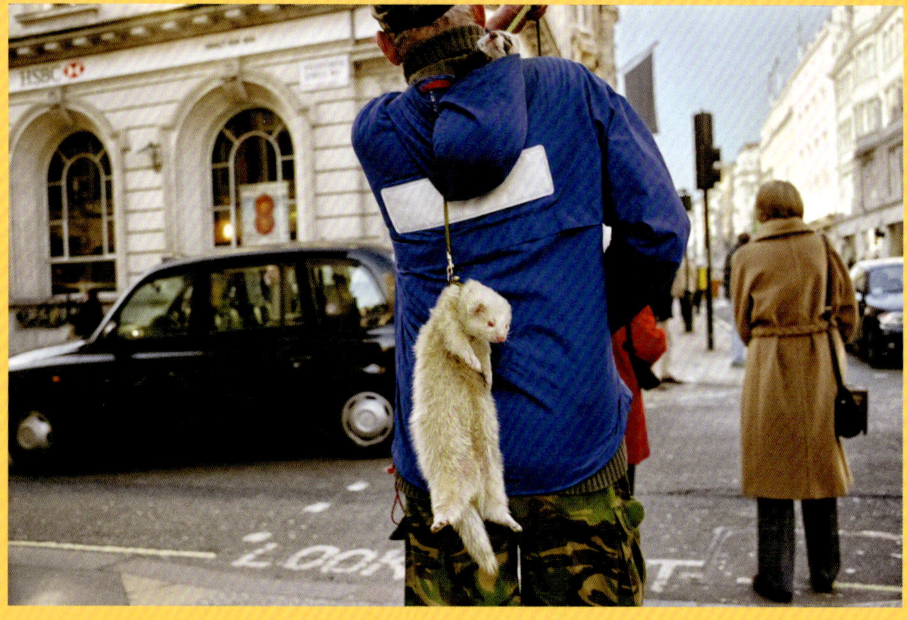

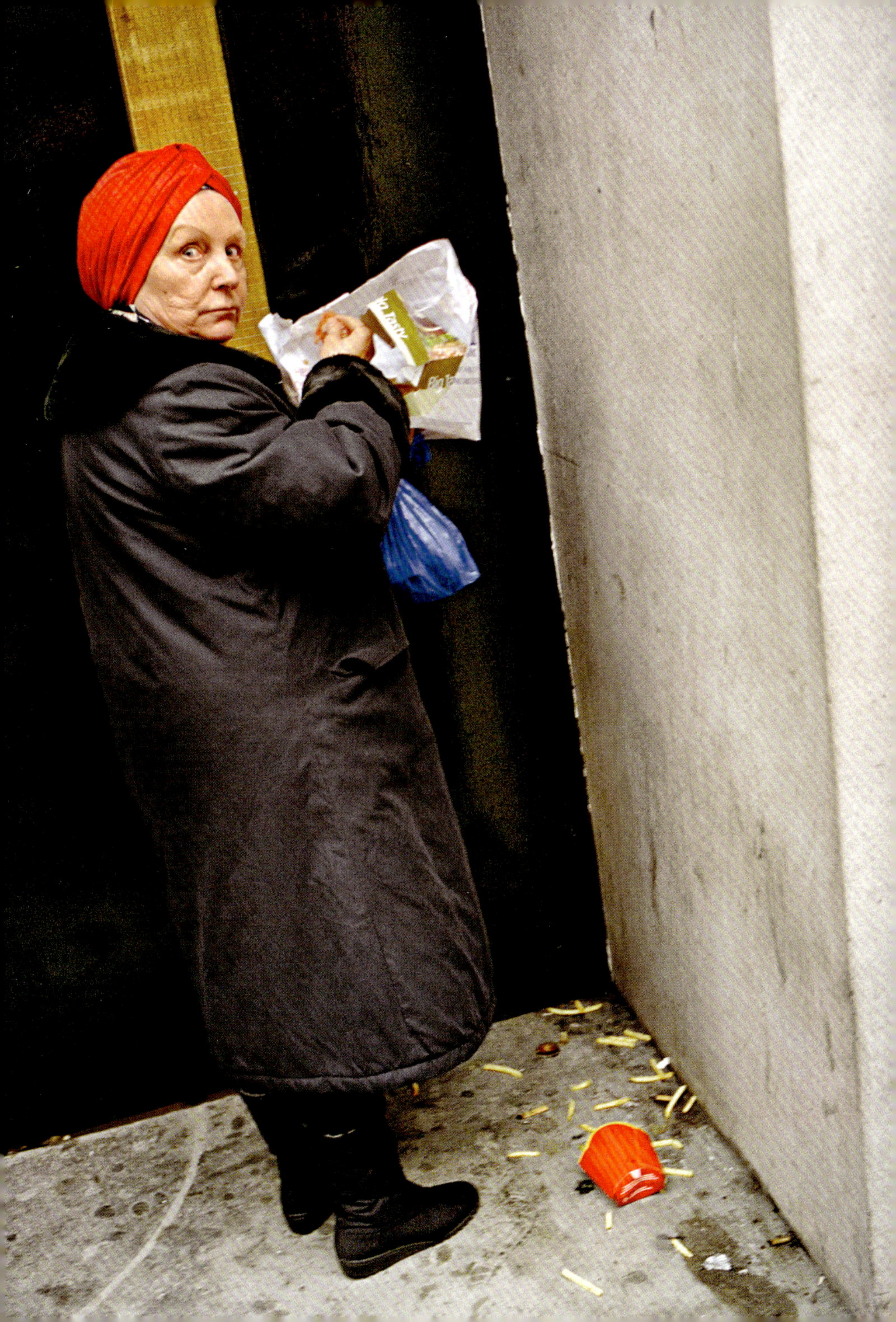

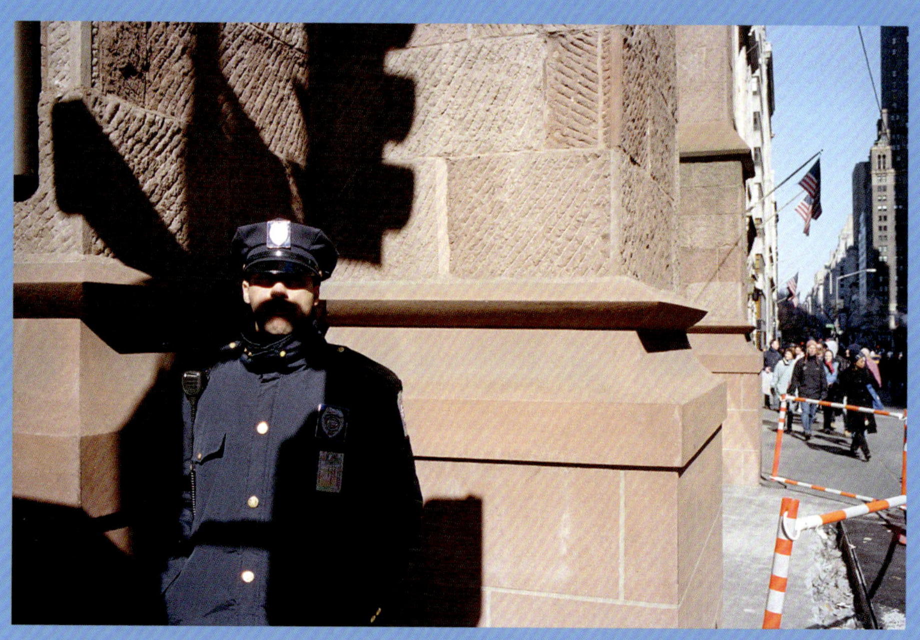

Fifth Avenue, New York, 2009

Chapter 10

THE THREE Fs

Fish, Follow, F**k!

The key to getting good pictures is threefold:
find a location that looks promising, track
something with potential, or jump straight in!

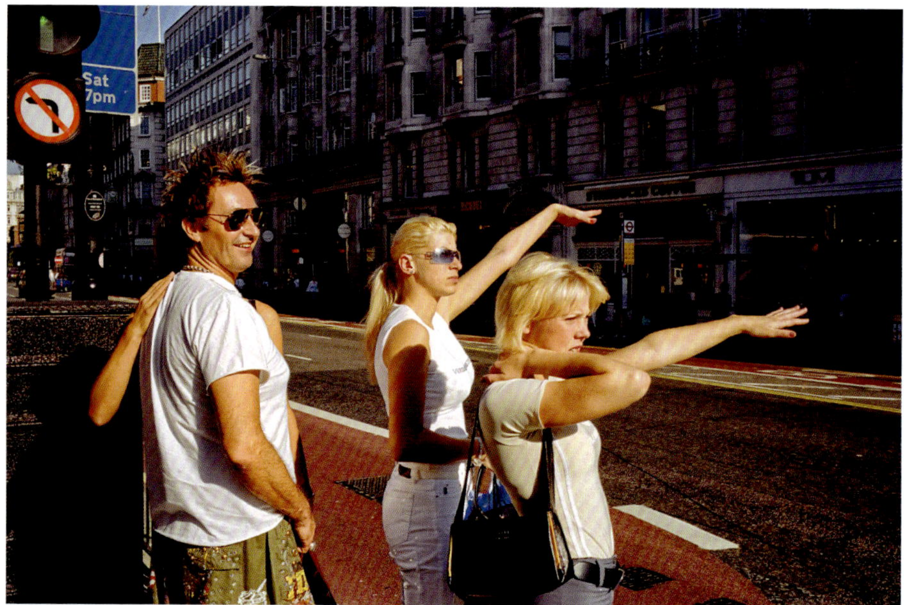

Piccadilly, London, 2007

A motto that has served me well over the years is 'The three Fs: Fish, Follow, F**k!' The most productive way of getting pictures is to find a place that is fruitful – somewhere with a good background, people and decent light – and wait for people to come to you. That's the 'fishing' hypothesis. It's an approach that doesn't involve moving around too much; you're just hanging out in your spot.

What can happen is, you clock something – a big fish swims past you – and you think, 'I'm going to jump in and swim after that fish'. That's the 'following' analogy: follow something with picture-making potential as it unfolds or develops. Don't think, 'I hope I've got it!' Run back and photograph it again. Each time you press the shutter, you're increasing your likelihood of getting a good picture.

The difficulty with 'following' is that the background constantly changes. Nine times out of ten the background will be the reason for the photograph failing. The 'F**k!' moments are the times you see something quite out of the blue and react without thinking too much – when a picture simply presents itself. The police officer picture on page 58 was one such moment. I walked past a church on Fifth Avenue in New York and saw the shadow on the officer's face.

'When you're in the moment, and this is just my view, you don't know what the decisive one is.'

The most difficult thing was putting the camera to my eye because he was a police officer, but he didn't say or do anything. Had he challenged me, I'd have said, 'There was an amazing shadow across your face and I love the light.' I was quite pleased with the picture – it's somewhere between

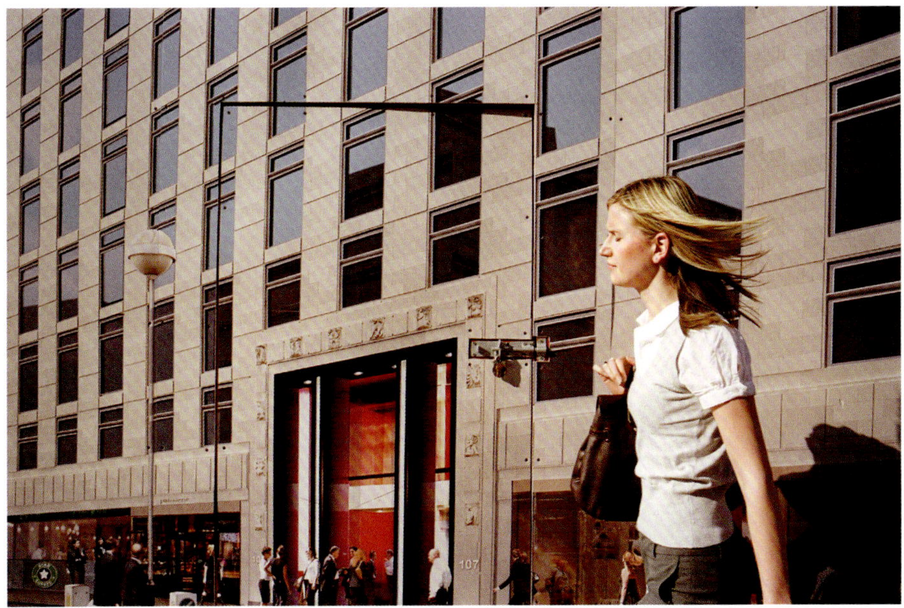

Poultry, London, 2010

the Village People's Glenn Hughes and the Keystone Kops.

When you see something that arouses your curiosity, photograph it as soon as you see it so you've got one picture and, if the situation allows, keep shooting through the moment even if you think you've already got the shot. That way, you're giving yourself options when you come to edit.

While I have endless respect for Henri Cartier-Bresson, who is one of my photography heroes, his idea that there is a 'decisive moment' can lead you to believe that there is always just one moment to capture a shot. In my experience, there might be three or four moments around the moment that is later labelled 'decisive'.

When you're in the moment, and this is just my view, you don't know what the decisive one is. You might hope for it, but you're going to try this and then that, or move a fraction one way or another.

It's actually at the editing stage, when you're scrutinizing each shot under a magnifier, that you decide which of the moments you captured is the decisive one. There is no shame in giving yourself as many chances as possible to catch the fish that attracted you.

The photograph overleaf is a 'fishing' picture. I was with a friend, the photographer Graciela Magnoni, and saw the poster of a girl on a bicycle with the strap-line 'Freedom to come and go', which seemed ironic given that several CCTV cameras were alongside it. I told Graciela that I needed some time. I was hoping to capture someone walking perfectly inside the bicycle wheel sculpture, so Graciela and I arranged to meet up later. This was just as well, because it took four hours before the lady in the blue dress walked into the scene and everything fell into place, and I could finally go and eat!

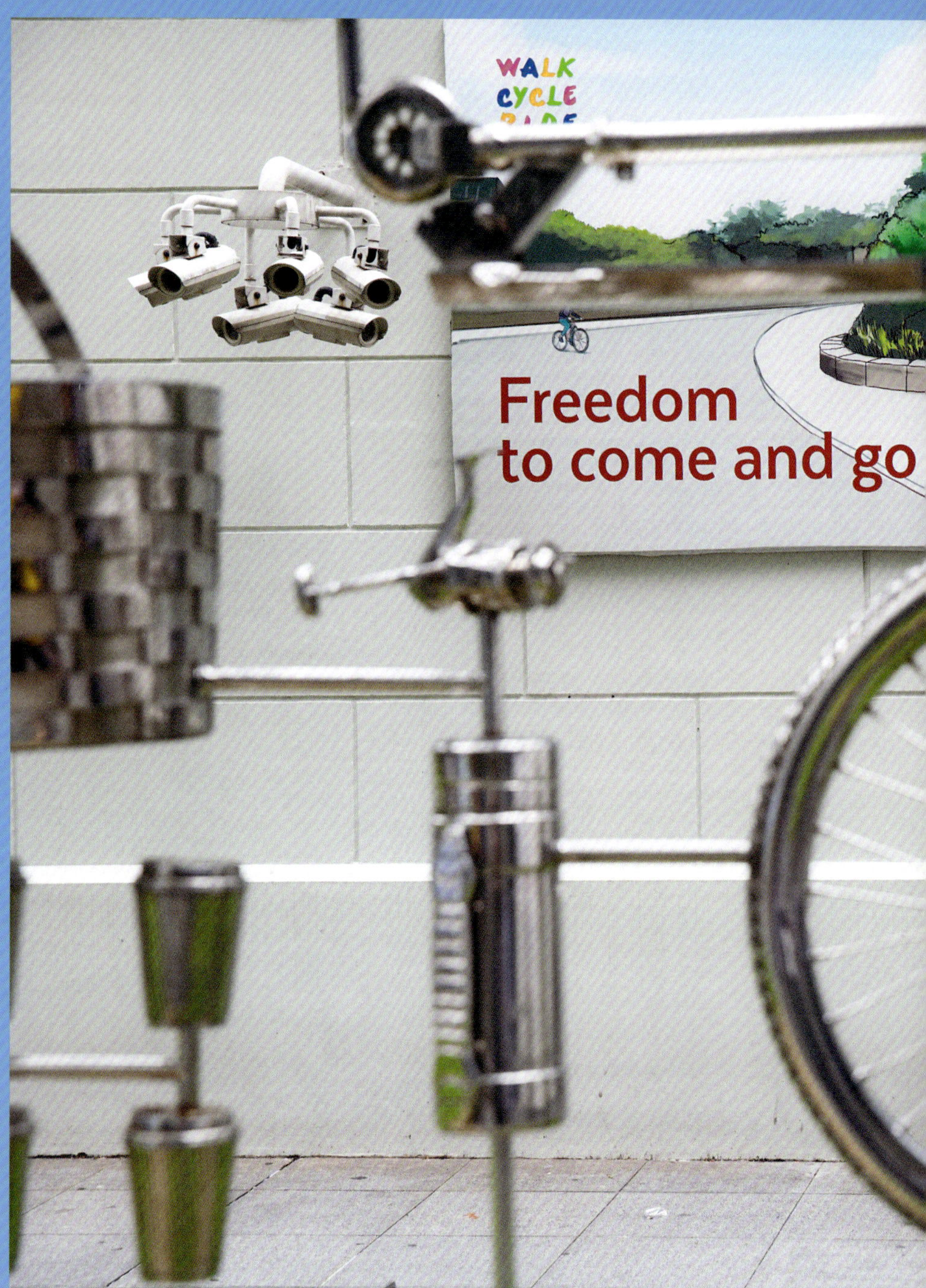

Singapore, 2017

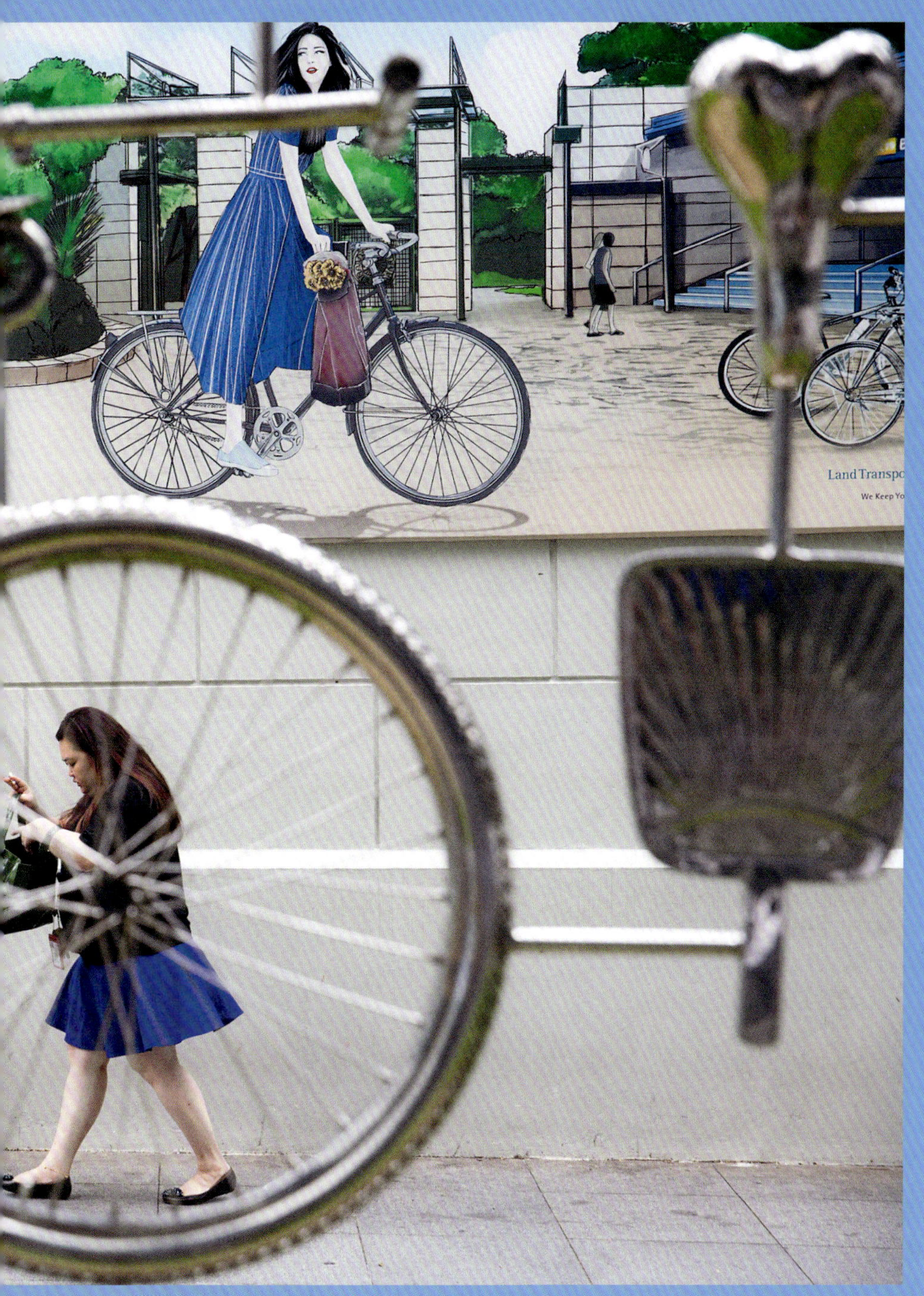

Land Transpo
We Keep Yo

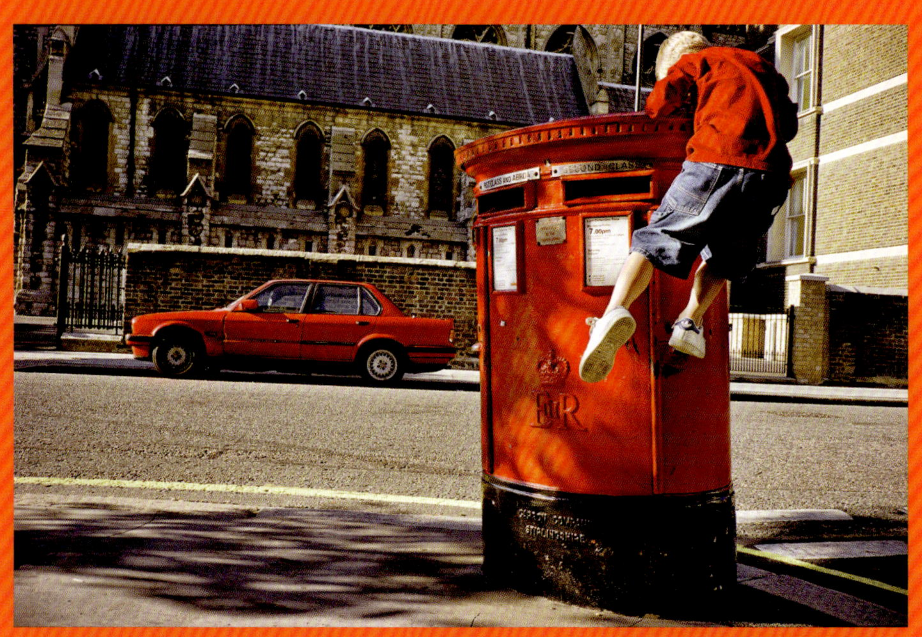

Needham Road, London, 2008

Chapter 11

STRANGE BUT TRUE

You wouldn't believe it!

Sometimes events can unfold before your eyes that you just couldn't make up. If you're alert and respond quickly, you'll make the shot. Don't hang around – take lots of exposures and check later whether you got it or not.

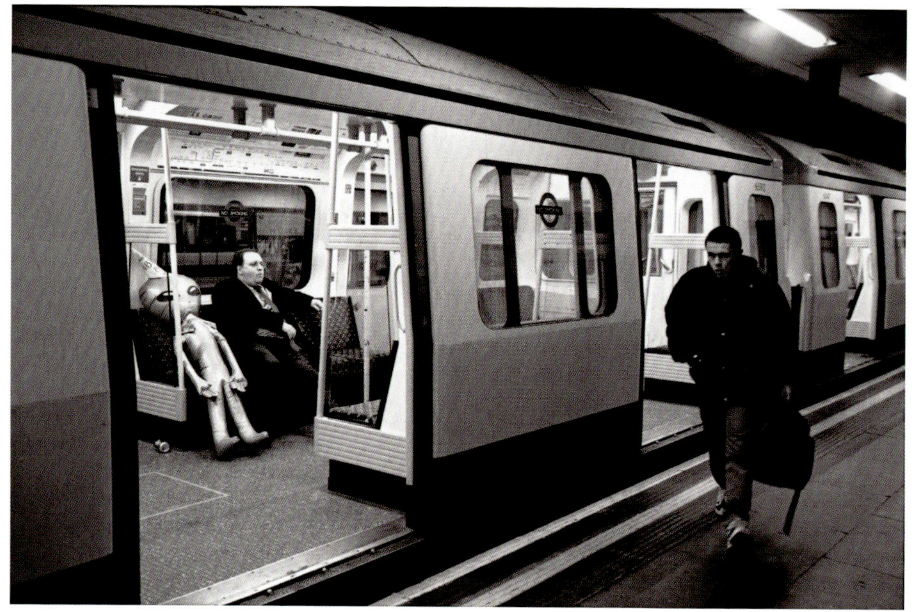

Moorgate Underground station, London, 2002

One of the many reasons I like street photography is that a lot of the time you can't imagine or plan what happens in public. Some things that life offers are far more interesting or revealing than anything you can make up. You might not have any control over how those moments happen, but you do have a degree of control over how you respond. It's about being alert and reacting fast.

In other types of photography, the photographer, perhaps a press photographer, goes out into the world to report

'Some things that life offers are far more interesting or revealing than anything you can make up.'

what is happening. Street photographers, on the other hand, play with people's expectations and make viewers question what they're looking at. You're not a reporter, you're in this slightly grey area of showing reality, but using ambiguity and surrealism to bend or distort what passes in front of the lens.

The kid in the picture on page 64 looks kind of superhuman, as though he is floating. In fact, he was jumping up, trying to get on top of the postbox, probably just to see if he could. I was sitting on a pub bench having a drink with some friends and had probably already subconsciously noticed the red postbox and the red car in the background. I had a really small camera with me and took two or three pictures, one of which worked. It was taken from a low angle looking up because I was sitting down when he jumped. Since the boy had tried to climb up first, and then had a go at pulling himself up, I had a few seconds to respond to what was going on. It was a mix of being really lucky, but also being switched on, having a camera with me and continually thinking about what might make a good image.

The close encounter with the alien opposite, who was taking the London Underground, is another example of why

'Street photographers... play with people's expectations... using ambiguity and surrealism to bend or distort what passes in front of the lens.'

it pays to keep your eyes peeled. I took the image at about eleven o'clock at night at Moorgate station, which is close to where I used to live. Again, it was down to having a camera with me at all times and always being on the look-out for pictures. The train pulled up, the doors opened and there was a man, who had had a good evening, sitting next to an alien. The doors stayed open for about a minute, so I was lucky and had time to shoot. The man just sat there having a nice chat with the alien and I had a camera to capture it.

The shot overleaf of a man in a devil costume standing alongside a driver whose car had been clamped I certainly couldn't have imagined or planned any better if I tried. The man in costume was being filmed for something and was taking a break. I'd got a couple of shots of him standing by the car, but when the driver arrived to examine his fine, it made the shot. The mischievous expression on the devil's face, the strange logo in the background and the huge green clamp in the foreground – all of those things, entirely coincidental as they were, came together to make the picture what it is.

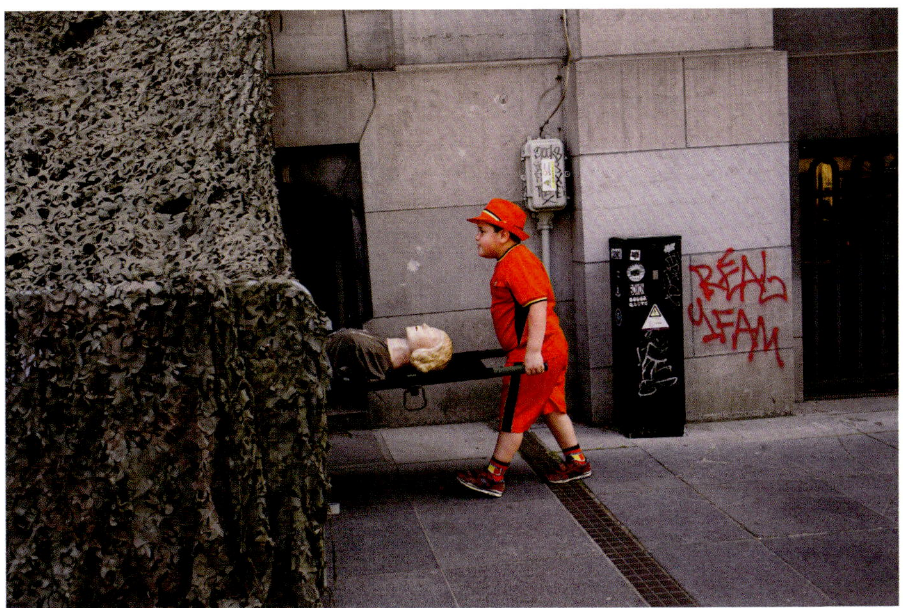

Brussels, 2016

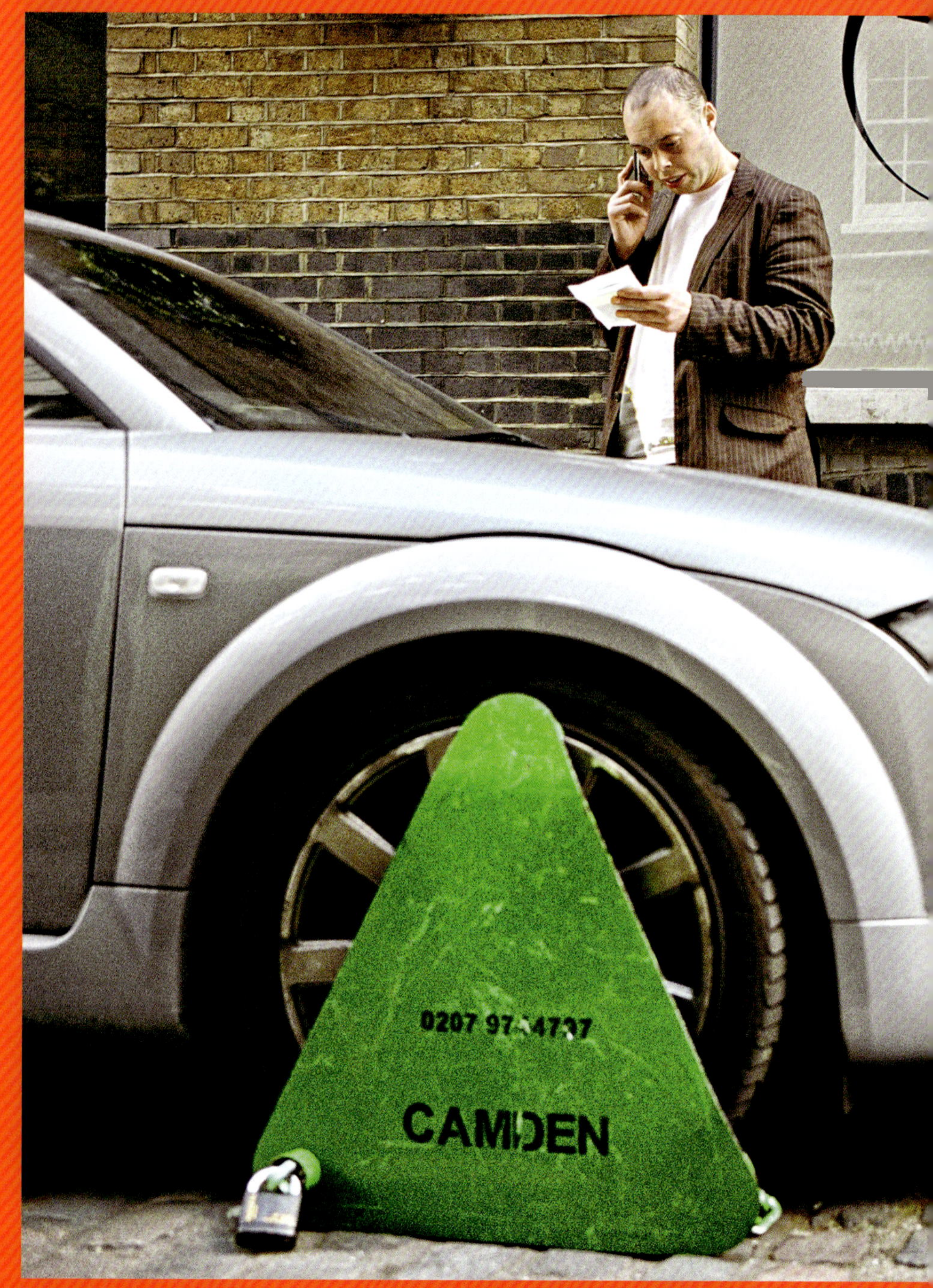

Shorts Gardens, London, 2010

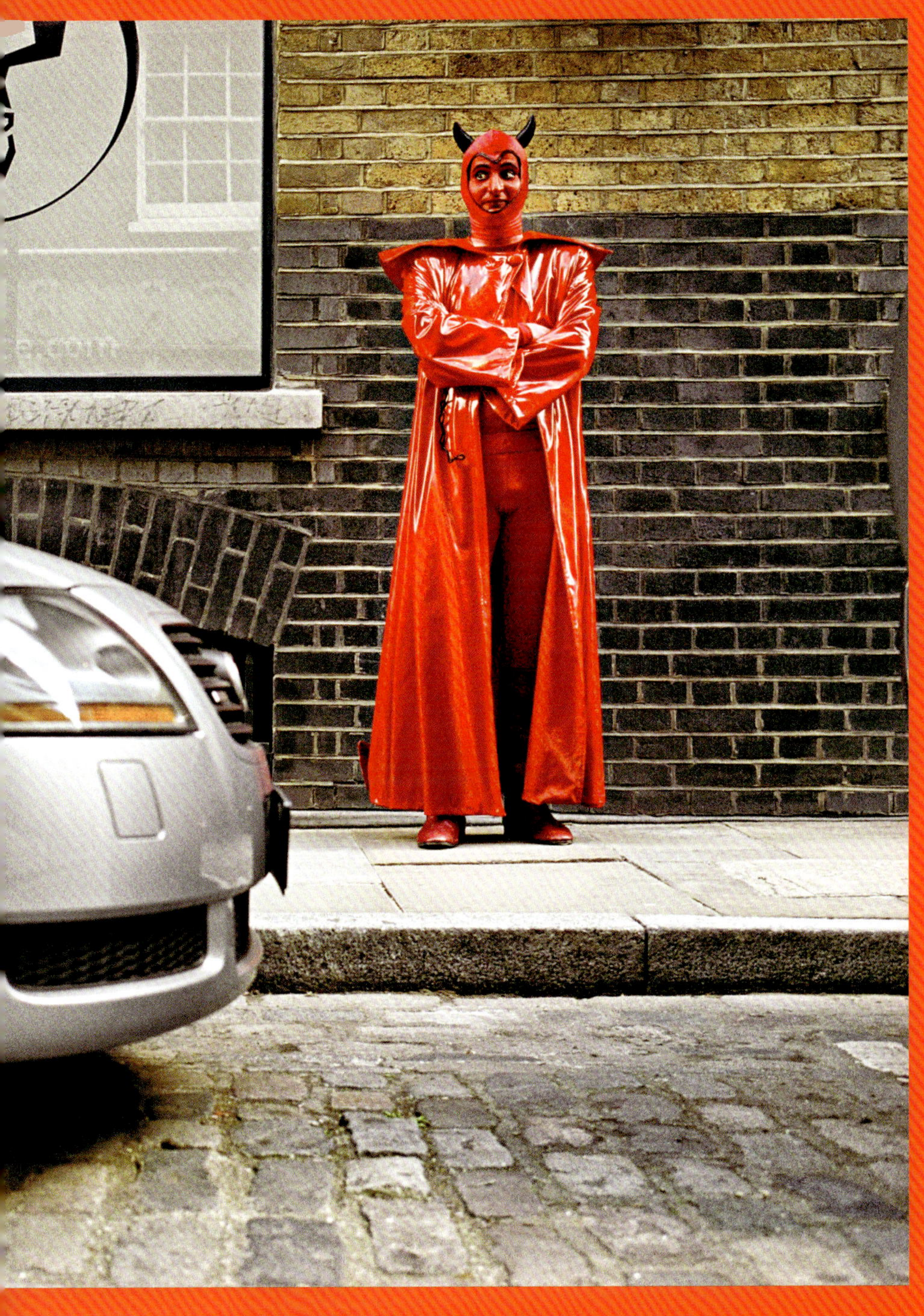

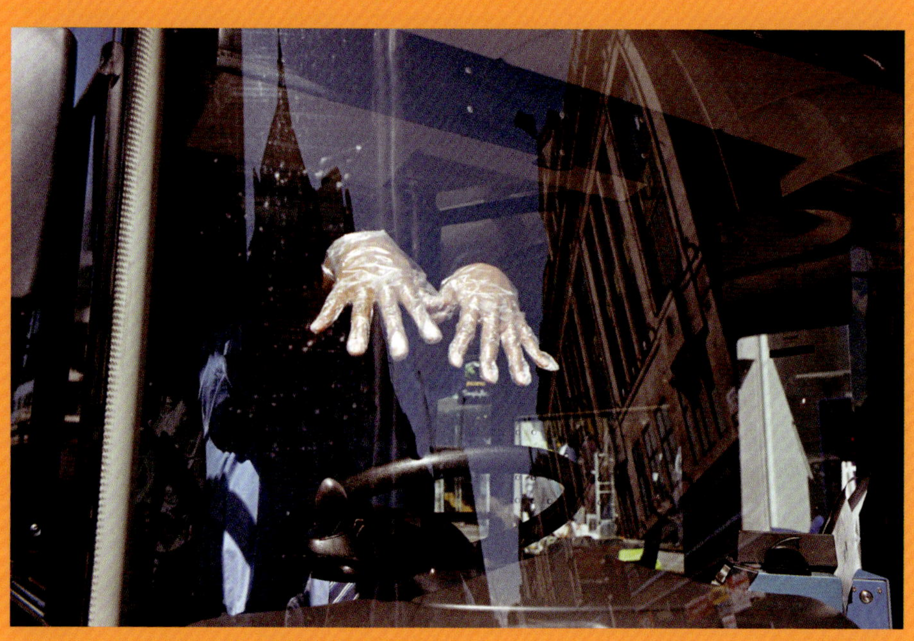

Oxford Street, London, 2016

Chapter 12

BE A FORTUNE TELLER

See the future before it happens

If you're switched on and alert, you can anticipate
events before they happen. With practice you
can learn to spot stories just as they appear
and begin to predict how they might unfold.

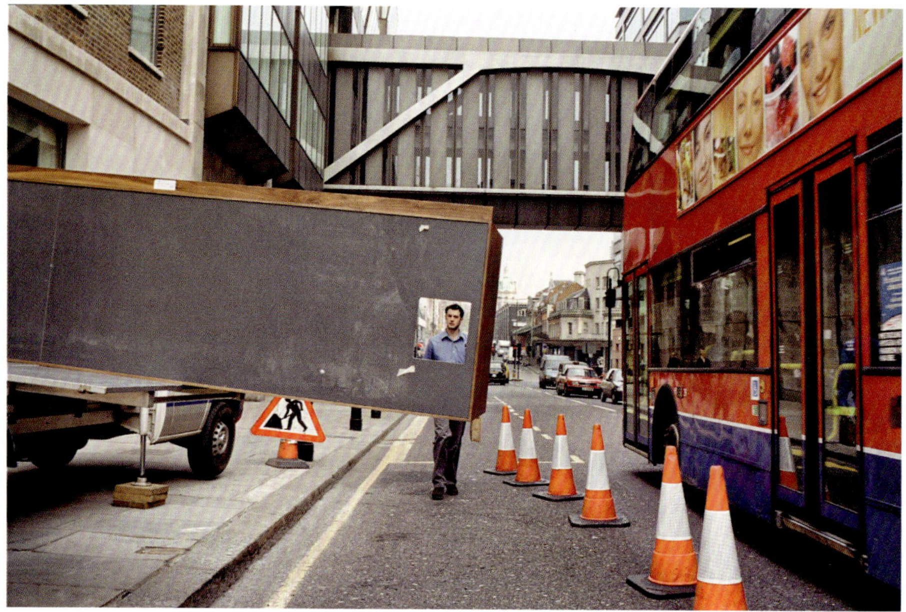

Charterhouse Street, London, 2008

don't have the ability to see into the future any more than the next photographer, but over the years I've learned how to spot things – mini narratives – before they happen and to second-guess how they might evolve.

As a photographer whose natural habitat is the street, one of the best experiences is when what you think is about to happen, does actually happen, and you're there to capture it. When I'm out, my eye is roving all the time, scouring everything in search of potential subjects. When I clock something that catches my attention, I wonder what might happen next and ask myself if it's worth the wait for a picture. All this happens very quickly and I do it automatically now. Sometimes I will follow an interesting subject with my eyes, trying to work out where he or she might go next or what they might do. It doesn't always lead to anything picture-worthy, but occasionally it pays off.

There is alchemy at work in the 'hands' picture on page 70, although once you know the story behind it, you realize it has everything to do with predicting what might happen rather than anything supernatural or magical. I like it because it has an air of sorcery and makes me think of a magician casting a spell, or the hands of a puppeteer or mime artist. In fact, they're the hands of a bus driver. The picture works because of the way the light is falling – everything except the hands is in shadow. Despite appearances, it wasn't a one-shot lucky catch. I took a couple of frames. To begin with the driver's hands were on the wheel and I found the plastic gloves he was wearing slightly bizarre. I was standing in front of the bus, which had stopped at traffic lights, and when the lights changed the driver shooed me out of the way. Because I've learned to pay attention to light and how it falls on subjects,

I saw that the gloves were illuminated but the background wasn't. The bus driver disappeared into the shadows. I was in that space for only a few seconds, but it was long enough to guess what might happen and react to it.

The picture of the upside-down boy below is a good example of when a moment of anticipation led to a noteworthy picture. It's quite a good story too. I was in Trafalgar Square and had spotted a man wearing headphones and dancing in front of The National Gallery. A bunch of schoolkids came by and started dancing with him. One of the kids was good at body popping and I overheard a conversation between him and another boy. 'Why don't you do a somersault?' said the other boy. The body-popper replied that he would have to practise on the grass first to warm up. I quietly followed them and the boy did a somersault, just one, and that's the picture. It was a one-click photograph.

I got the shot because I had overheard the boys' conversation and knew what they were going to do. I was prepared, almost as if the moment were scripted.

If you're looking, listening and anticipating, it is possible to be semi-psychic. Have the foresight to notice, stop, wait and visualize and use what's around you in creative ways.

TRY THIS

As the American photographer Walker Evans famously said: 'Stare, pry, listen, eavesdrop. Die knowing something. You are not here for long.'

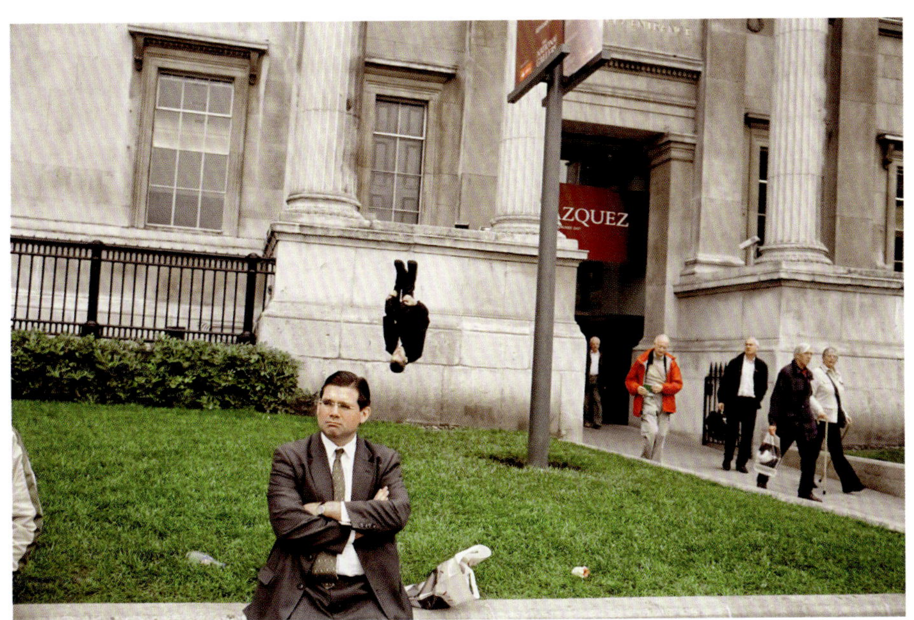

Trafalgar Square, London, 2007

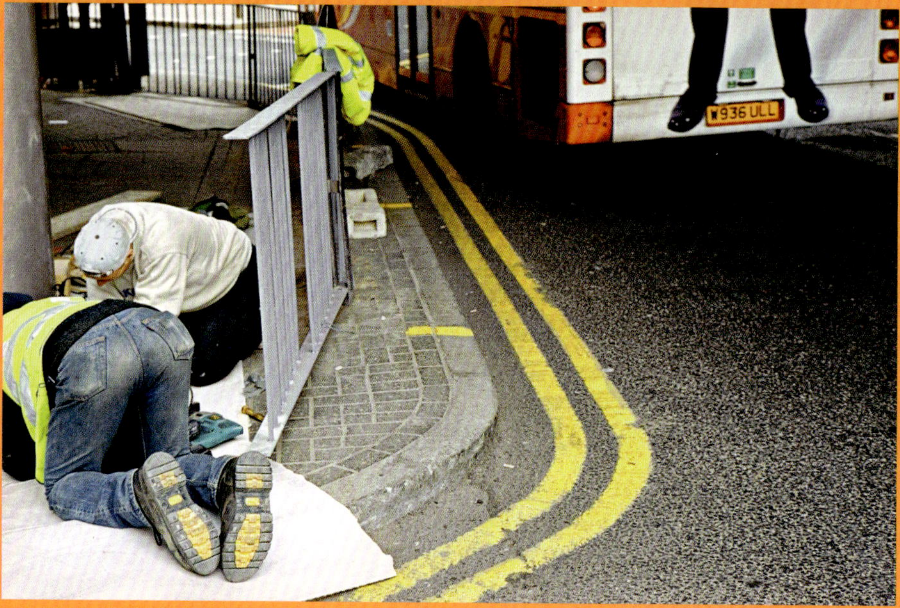

Drake Street, London, 2007

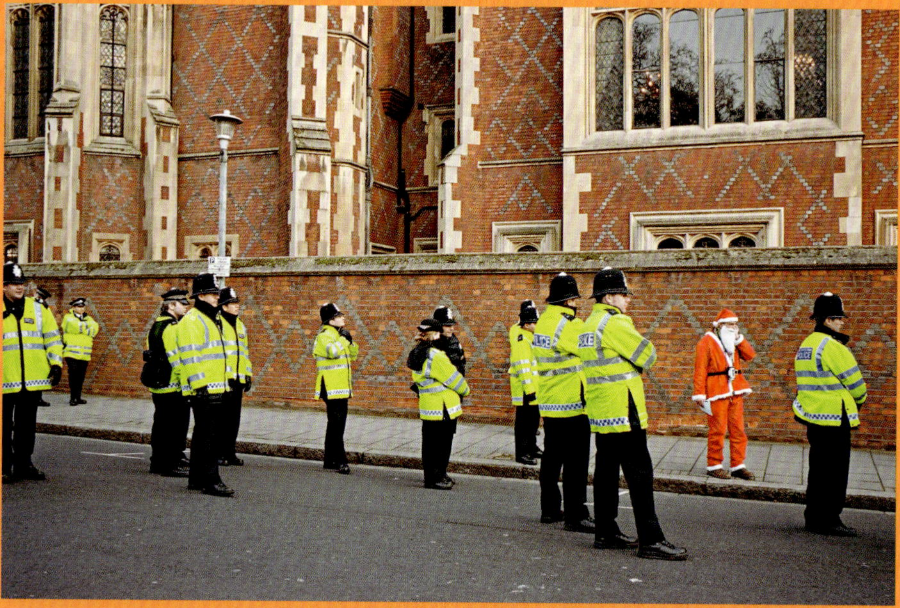

Lincoln's Inn Fields, London, 2006

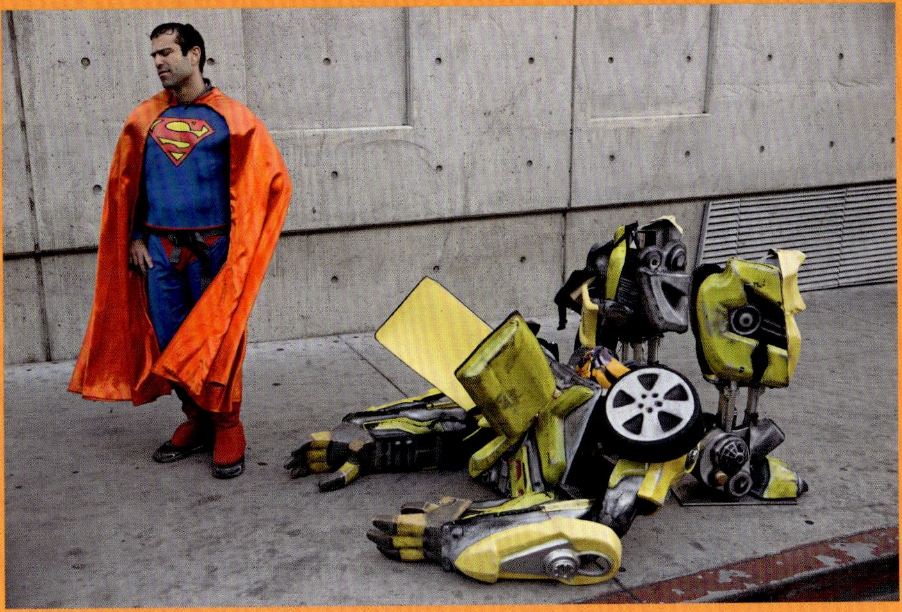

Hollywood Boulevard, 2017

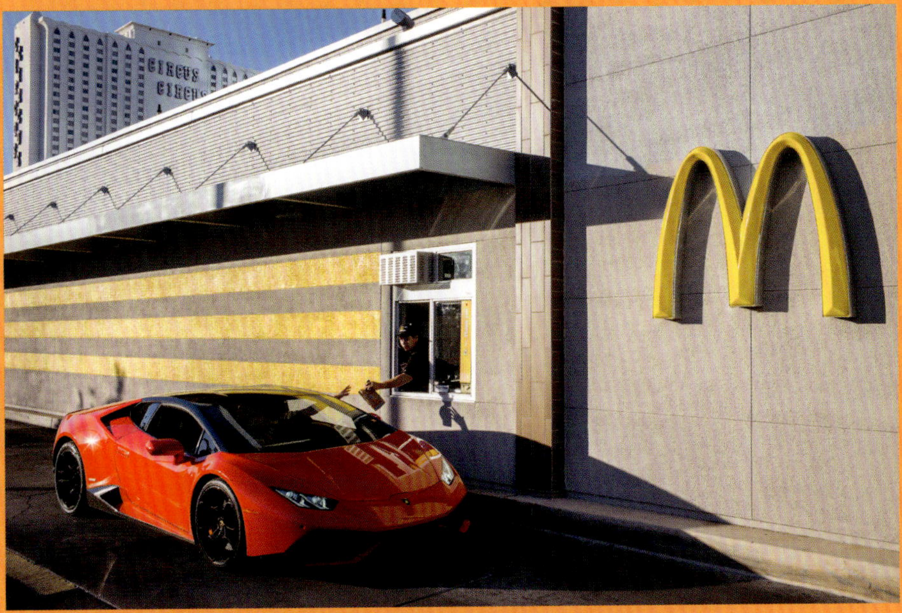

Las Vegas, 2017

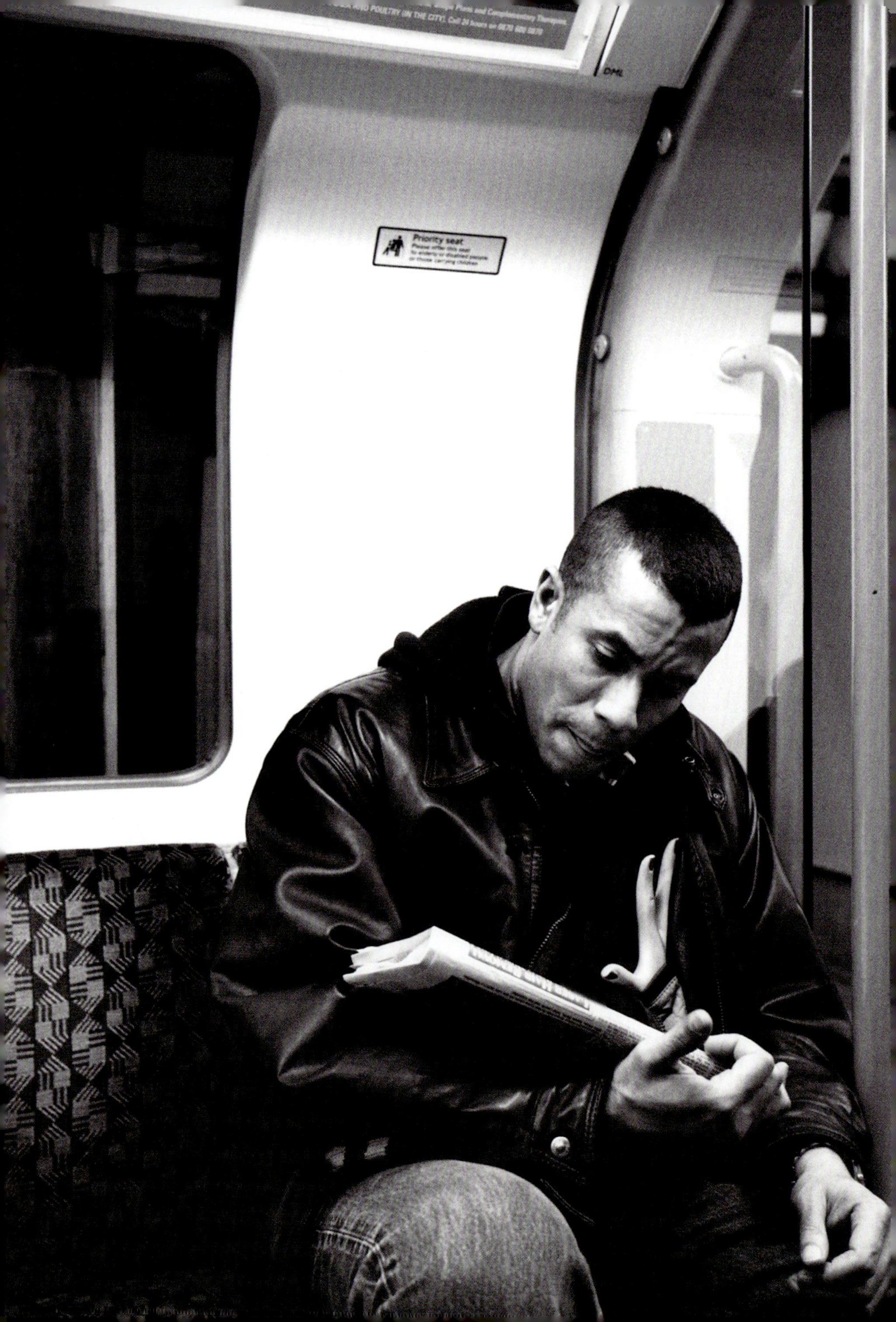

Priority seat
POULTRY IN THE CITY. Call 24 hours on

Chapter 13

TO SPEAK OR NOT TO SPEAK?

Knowing when to engage with your subject

Sometimes it's OK to get close and sometimes it's better to hang back, but that's a judgement call that is not always easy to make. If your intentions are good and you are unobtrusive who can argue with that?

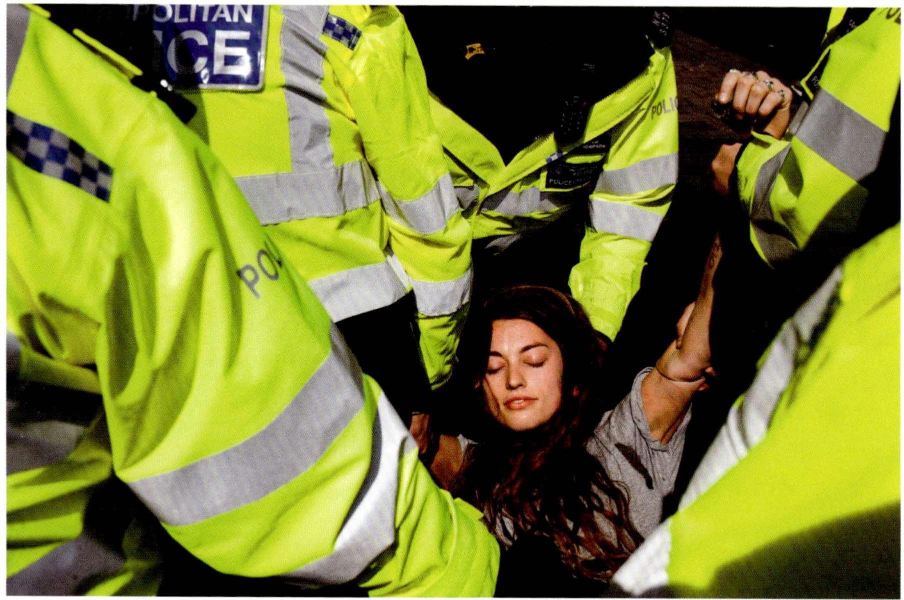

Page 76 Bank Underground station, London, 2001   **Above** Regent Street, London, 2019

Generally speaking, I don't engage with subjects. It's just what works for me. There are times, however, when you think, 'This is a great situation. Damn, I've been spotted! Perhaps speaking with that person is the thing to do and maybe a few words won't alter the picture too much… it could even help.' How you make that call comes down to what feels right at the time and depends on the situation.

Quite early on in my photography career, I encountered a man on the London Underground with a severed hand (page 76) and my life semi-flashed before my eyes. Well, no, that's not exactly what happened. It was a mannequin's hand, and I don't know why he had it, but I was afraid something bad might happen to me because the man was behaving quite strangely. Nonetheless, my curiosity was awoken.

It's not a brilliant picture, but the story's good, and it was quite a big moment for me in terms of getting over the fears I had about what might happen when photographing in public. It's also a good example of when speaking a few well-chosen words with confidence can help

'The good news is that knowing when… to engage and when to keep quiet… can be practised and learned.'

ease a potentially tricky situation. The man was standing on the platform at about half past ten at night, talking to himself and waving the mannequin's hand around. I couldn't let the moment pass without trying to get a picture.

I'd been taking photographs on the Underground regularly for a couple of weeks at this point because I was trying to capture a shot of a sleeping person underneath a particular poster (page 33). Consequently, I knew what the exposure would be (1/60 sec at f/2.8 at ISO 800 constantly, since it would be under the same light). I also knew how far away a person sitting opposite would be, so I could pre-focus. As I raised my camera to my eye, the man put the hand into his pocket so it was just peeking out. On the third frame he caught me taking his picture. Frozen inside but calm on the outside, I told him I liked the mannequin hand, which was true. He said thanks, and carried on reading. That was it. My worst fears had not been realized.

On this occasion, it made complete sense to say a few words – to be honest and direct about my intentions without over-engaging. I got an OK picture, but, more importantly, I learned that sometimes engaging just briefly with a subject is the best thing to do, especially in tricky situations. My confidence grew a hundredfold.

The good news is that knowing when and how to make this judgement call – deciding when to engage and when to

'The more you shoot in public... the more used you will become to making lightning-speed moral judgements about when and when not to engage.'

keep quiet – can be learned and practised. The more you shoot in public and feel comfortable being around people with your camera, the more used you will become to making lightning-speed moral judgements about when and when not to engage.

Something related to this, although slightly different, is that there is a quandary

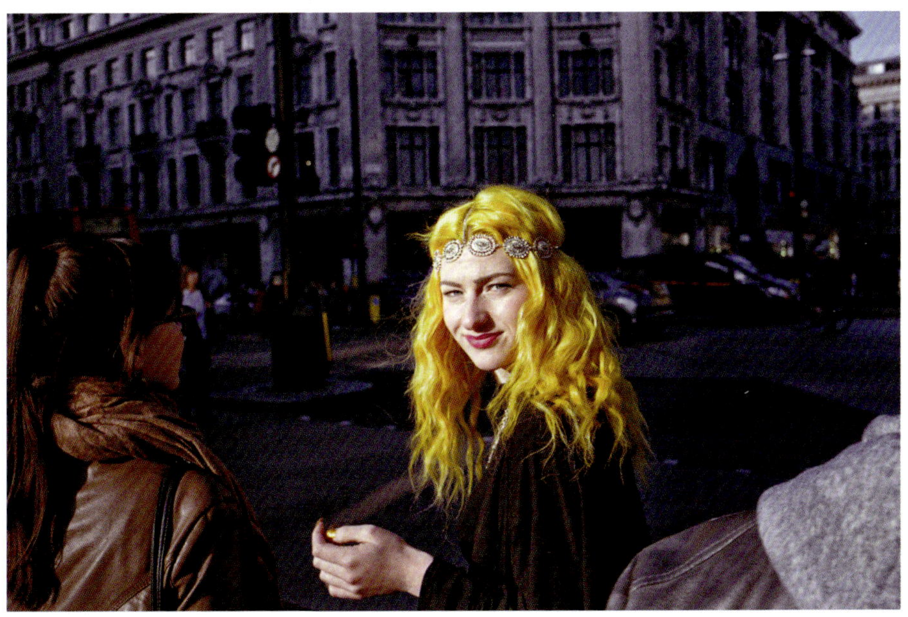

Oxford Circus, London, 2015

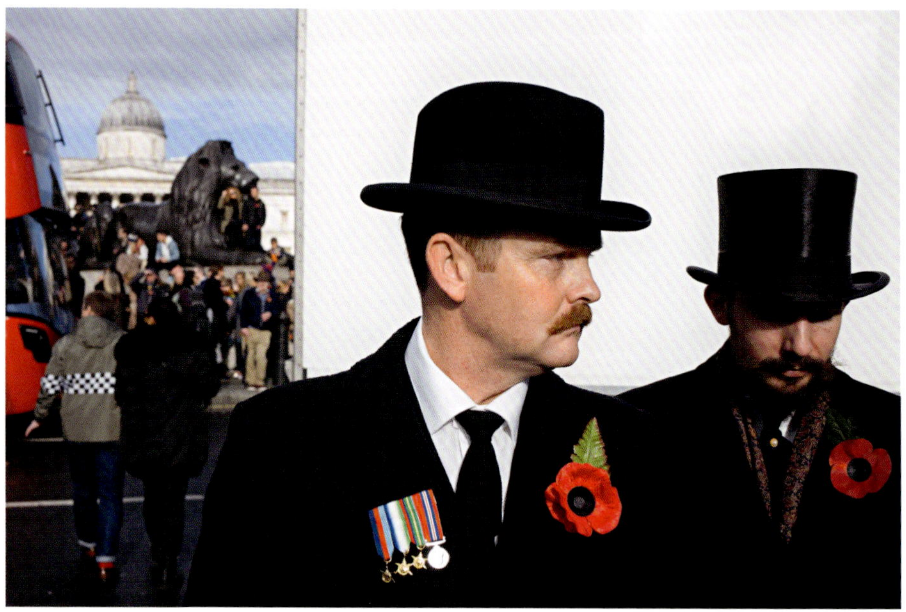

Trafalgar Square, London, 2018

that comes when deciding how close to get to a subject – namely, how to develop a sense of what's acceptable in terms of being in a person's space. I'll often be within a hair's breadth of

'There is a quandary that comes when deciding how close to get to a subject – namely, how to develop a sense of what's acceptable in terms of being in a person's space.'

the person I'm photographing, and they won't know I'm there, but there are occasions – such as when there are fewer people around or when individuals have their own space – when it's difficult to blend in. In a park, for example, you tend to find pockets of people, or individuals, within the larger public whole, and if you try to approach can-

didly, you'll likely, although not always, to be seen from a mile off.

While there is a history of many street photographers not speaking to their subjects, there are some – such as Garry Winogrand, Helen Levitt and Joel Meyerowitz – who will engage with them when necessary in order to get the shot. An example is the picture opposite. The man caught me photographing him smoking, so I smiled, complimented him on his hair and asked whether I could continue. He was fine with that and carried on smoking. If I'd stuck to a candid 'don't speak' approach, the photograph would not have been made.

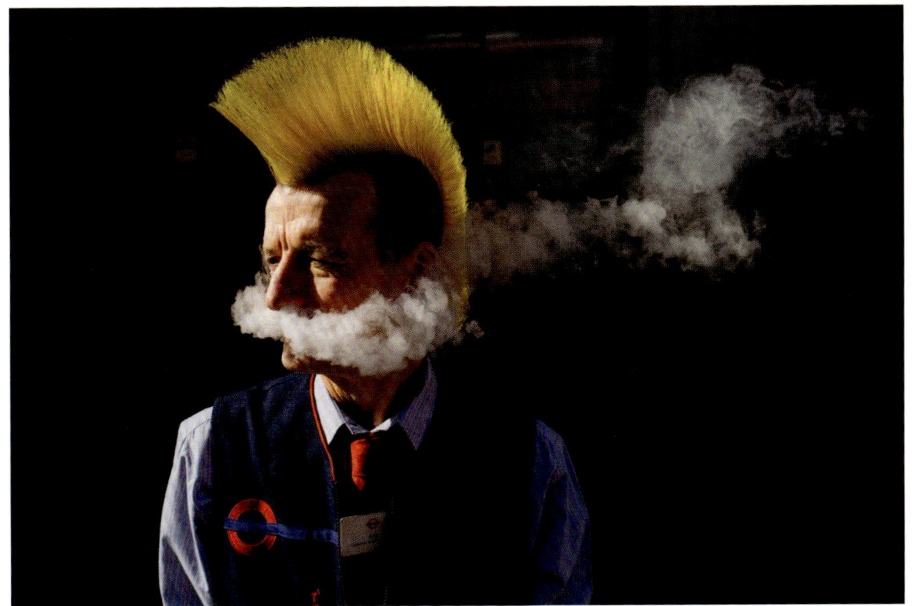

Oxford Circus, London, 2018

TRY THIS

Approach your subject if the situation
warrants it. Authenticity needs to be
in your approach, whether you engage
with your subject or not.

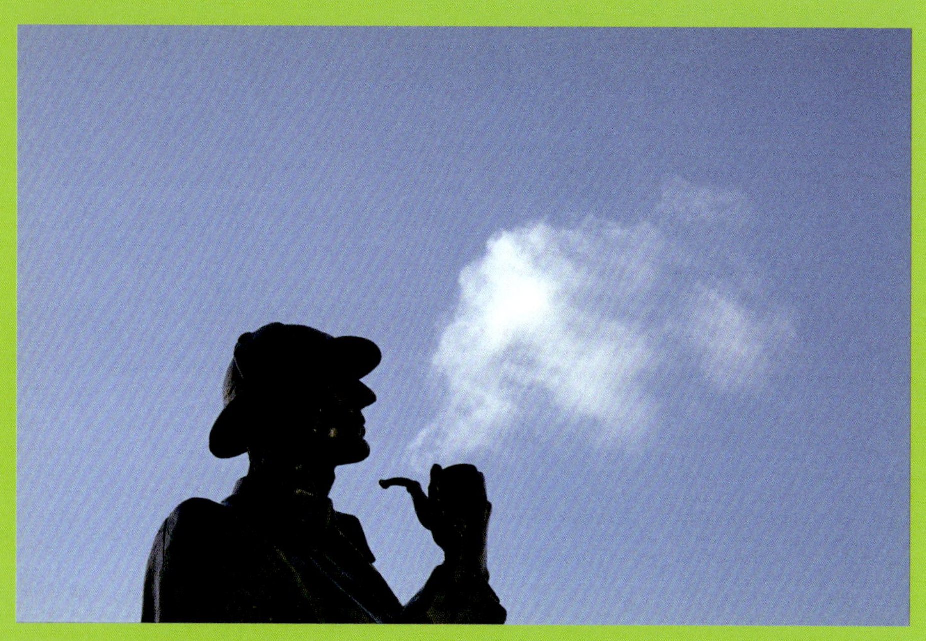

Marylebone Road, London, 2011

Chapter 14

TEN POINTS FOR A PIPE

Look out for certain objects or gestures

Photo-worthy subjects can be found everywhere on the street, though photographing them in a way that makes them look interesting takes practice. Looking out for specific motifs or themes can help you to focus your eye and mind.

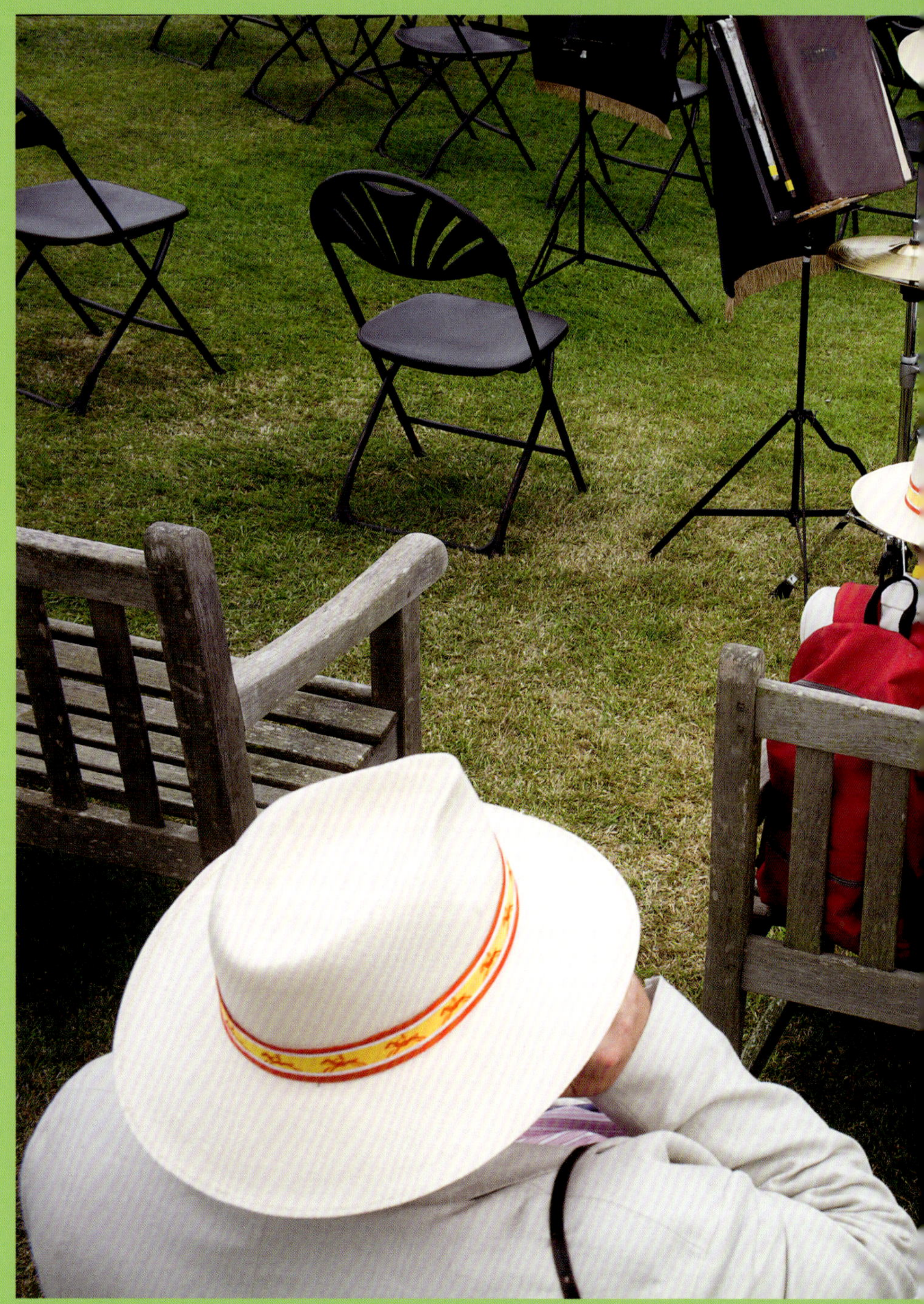

Glorious Goodwood Festival, Chichester, 2015

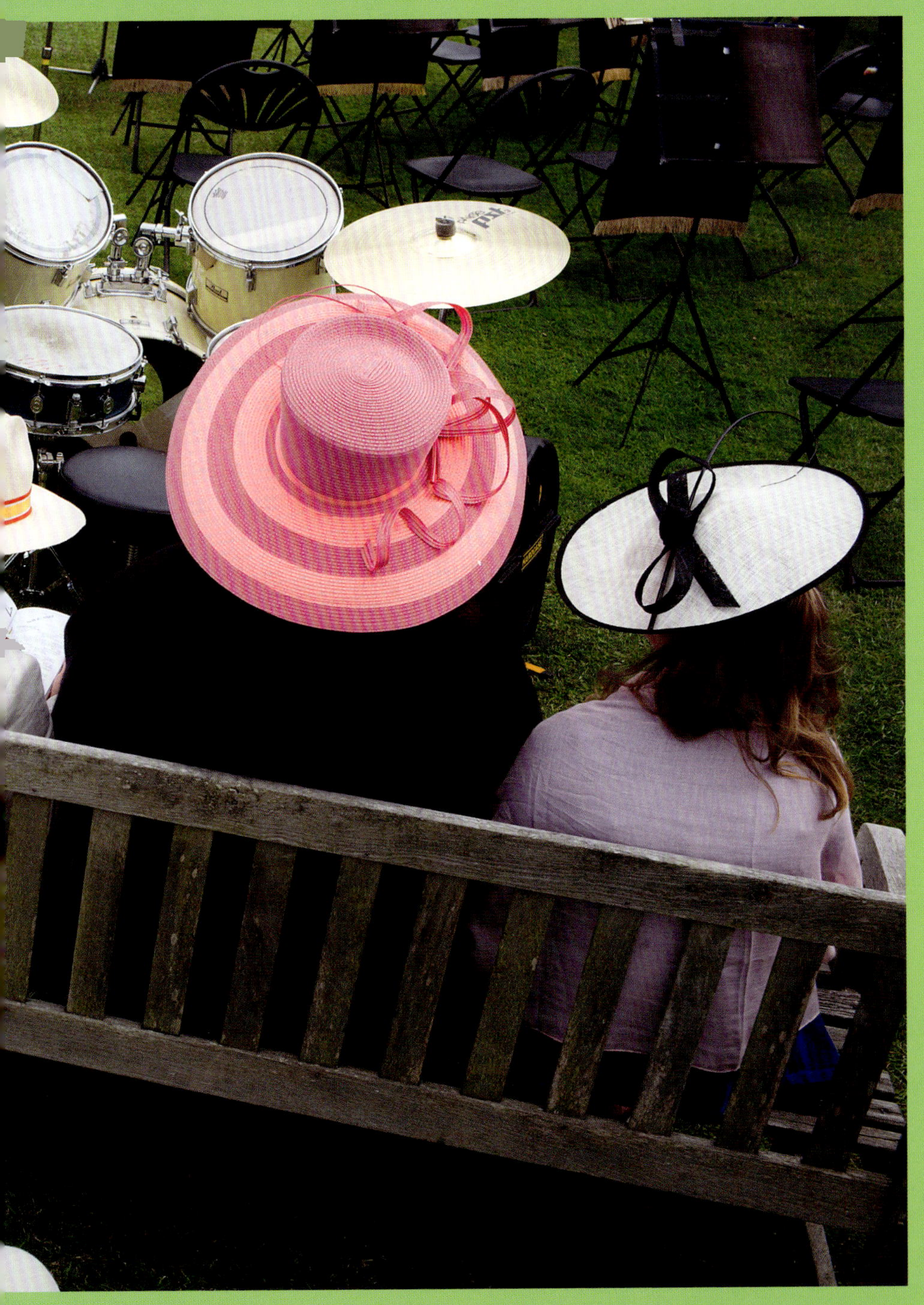

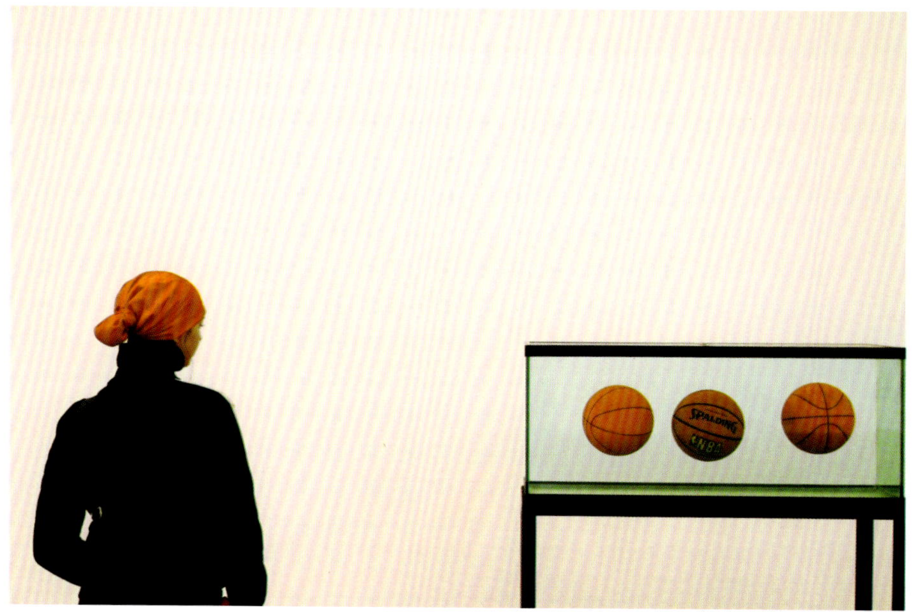

Tate Modern, London, 2002

You don't often see pipe smoking in public anymore, which is a good thing, but because it is a less common sight, when you do spot someone puffing away it leaps out. The same goes for bowler hats and cigars, handlebar moustaches, braces, feather boas, and so on.

I'm hard-wired to spot combinations of shapes and colours – from bright yellow road markings to red-rimmed road signs, postboxes and buses – and sometimes, early on in a shoot day as I'm getting into my flow, I subconsciously find myself looking for these triggers. While there's a danger of getting carried away with what I call 'graphic bullshit', which can get a bit gimmicky, it can be a useful way to fire up your creativity.

Spotting photo-worthy subjects is one thing, but making an interesting picture is quite another. What can help is 'sketch-ing' – playing with ideas by shooting and not thinking too much. You might photograph a scribble on a wall or a plastic bag that's made a strange shape. It doesn't matter if it's not perfect because it's a sketch. It comes back to how you 'reach' for a picture. A stretch here or a stretch there, a little jog here or a leap there – it all helps you to be ready for the picture that matters. Most photographs are sketches

'Spotting photo-worthy subjects is one thing, but making an interesting picture is quite another.'

or scribbles, and not everything is worthy of a gold frame, so embrace the sketch!

You can spot posters or elaborate shop fronts, which can make brilliant back-drops, all over London, or indeed in any town or city. Try looking for these and

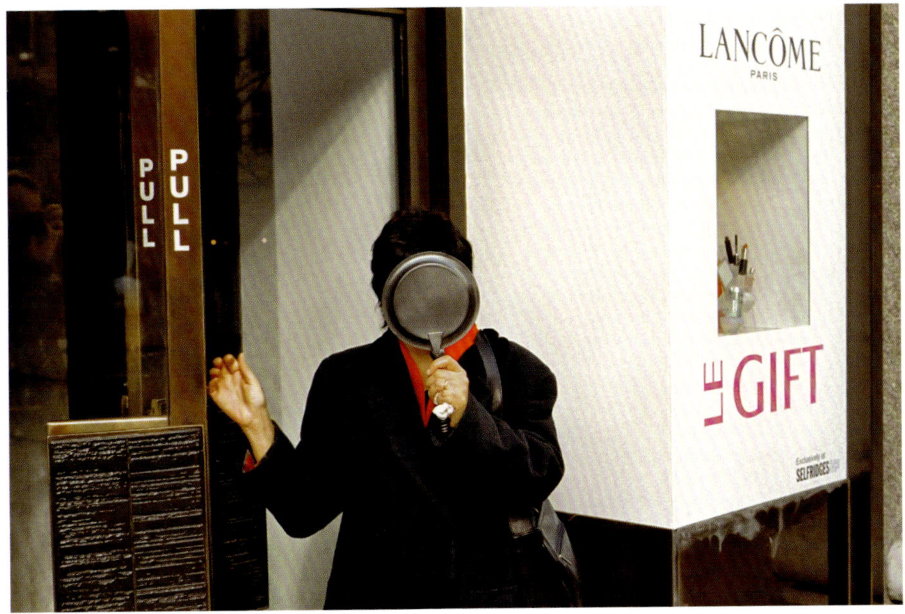

Oxford Street, London, 2007

see if you can use them in a composition, just for fun. Remember, you're not aiming for a killer shot – you're just sketching, playing. Henri Cartier-Bresson was a master of using backgrounds in clever ways. He would pick those that were interesting in their own right, and wait for his subjects to pass through, clicking the shutter when everything came together in the frame. In this way, his images were both lucky *and* the result of careful planning and seeing.

Approaching the street in this way – searching for specific motifs or themes – doesn't have to be something you do all the time, but it might give you a boost or a renewed sense of purpose, which we all need every now and again.

TRY THIS

Set tasks for yourself, collect stuff! Ten points if you can spot a pipe smoker. One point for someone on their phone. Try to stay awake!

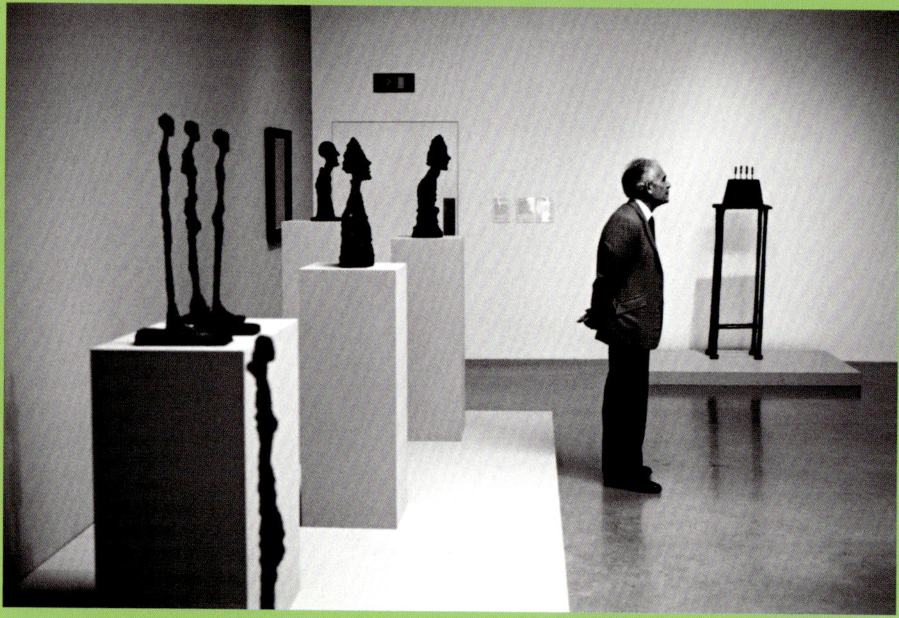

Tate Modern, London, 2000

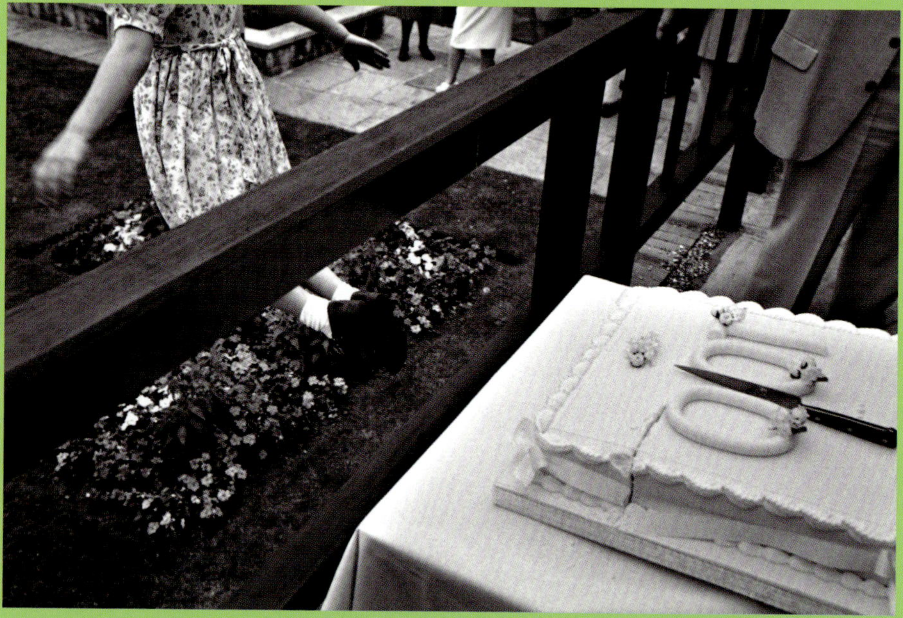

Bromley, London, 2000

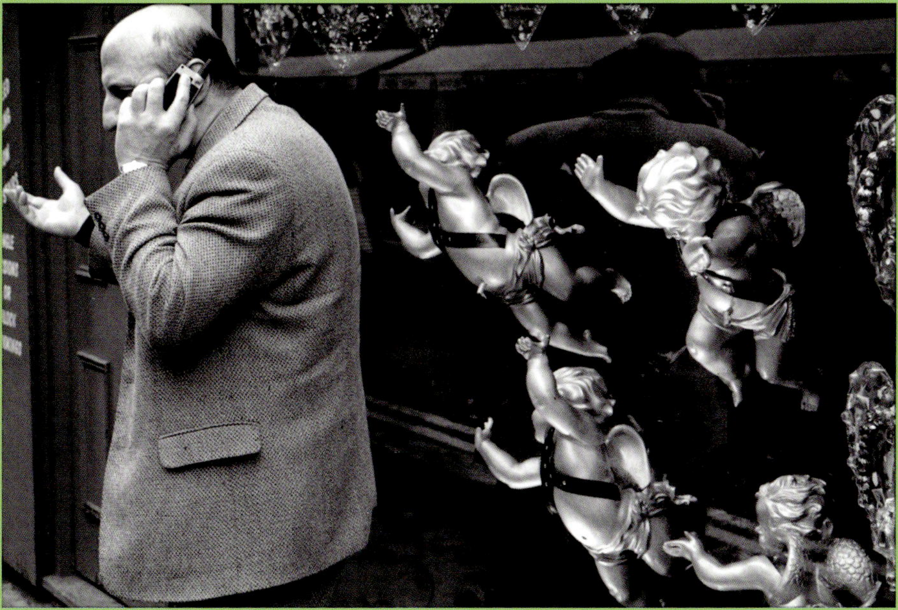

Old Compton Street, London, 2001

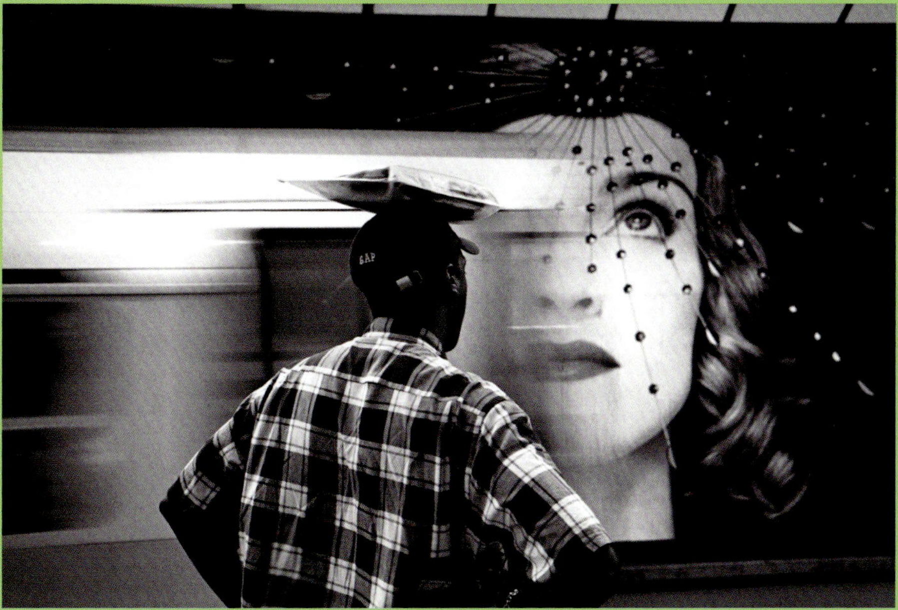

Moorgate Underground station, London, 2001

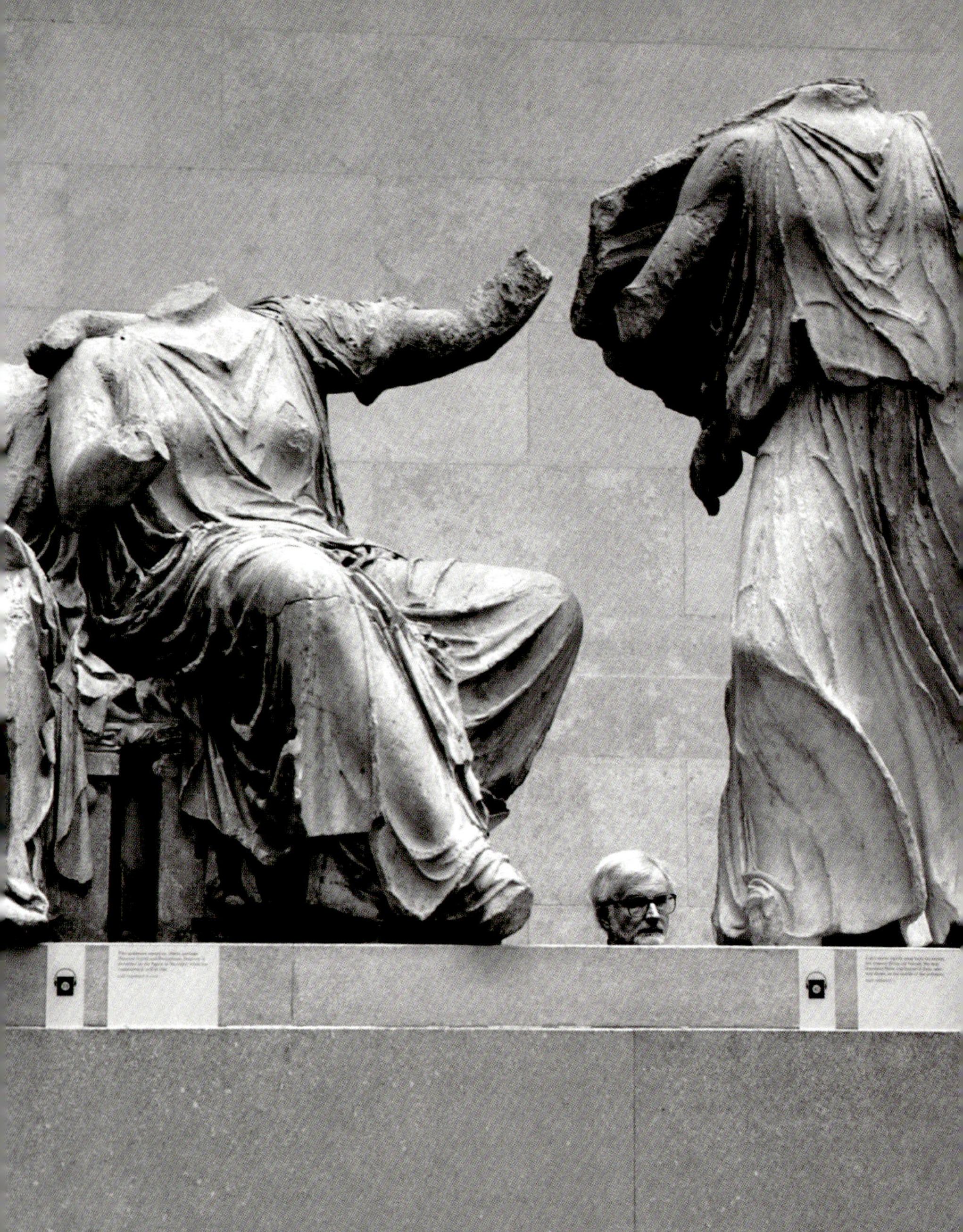

HA HA BONK!

Jokes and juxtapositions

Funny pictures don't just happen; they are the
result of practice and revisiting the same scene.
I'm all for one-liners, but they have to be good.

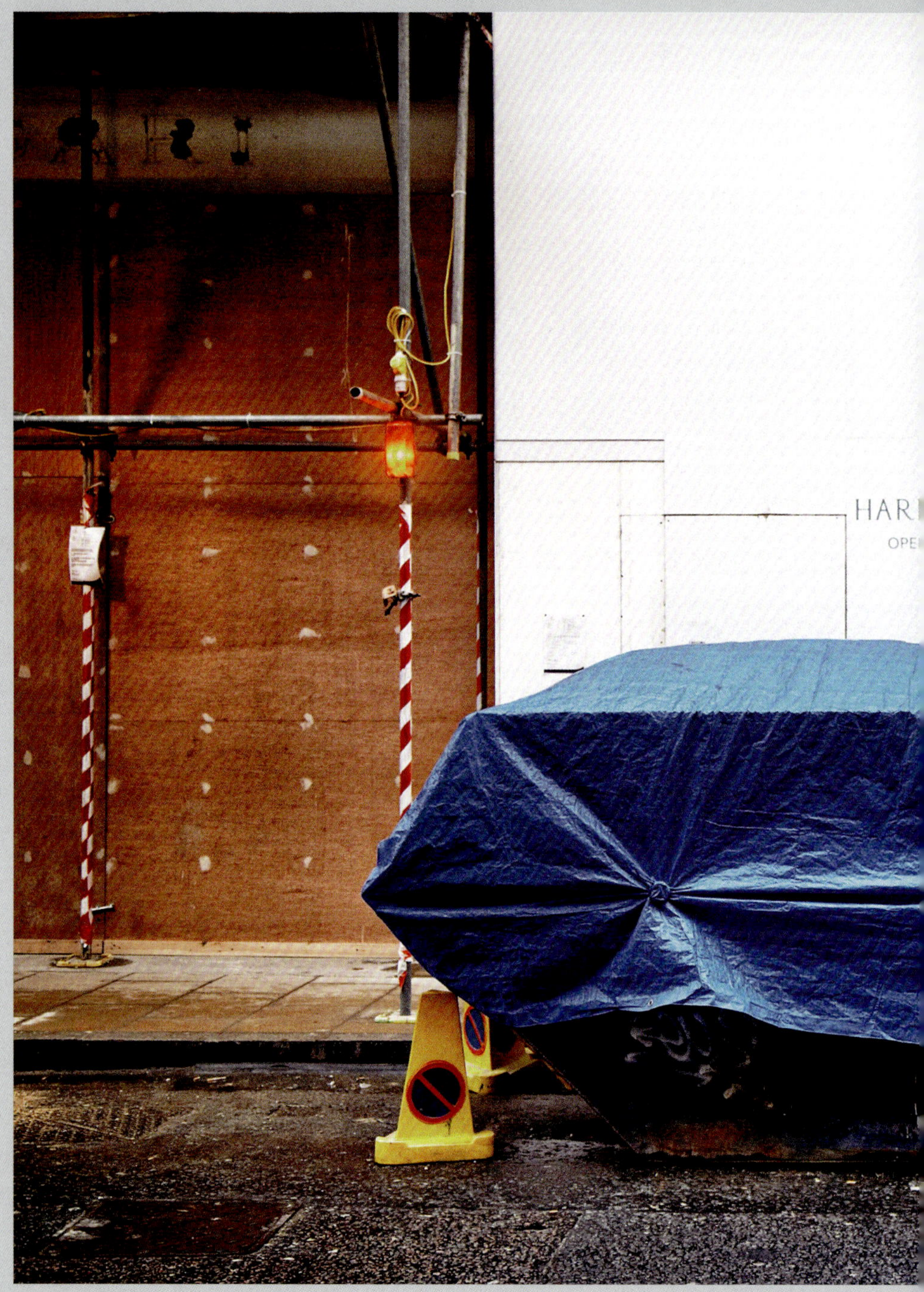

Previous pages British Museum, London, 2002   **Above** New Bond Street, London, 2006

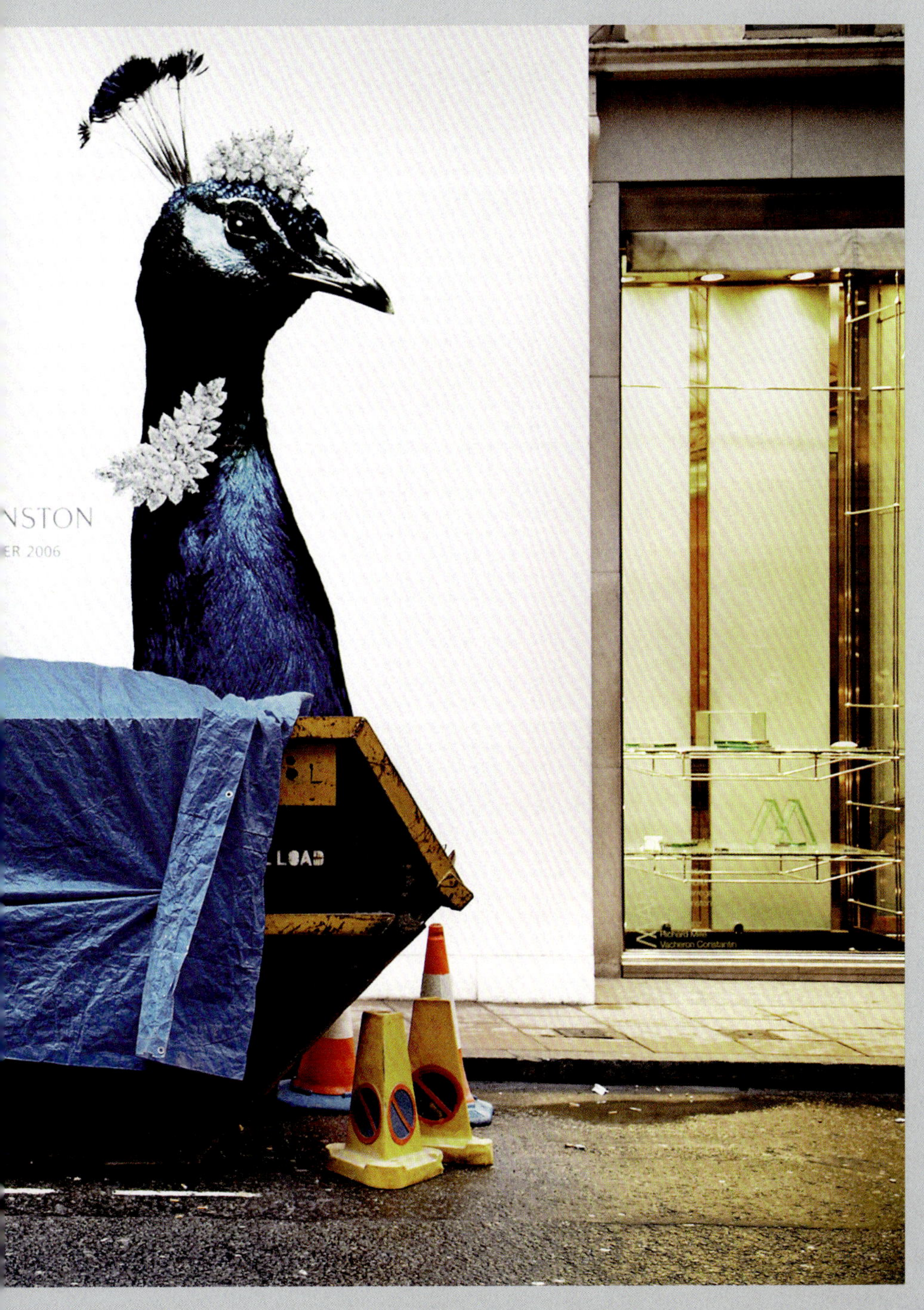

NSTON
ER 2006

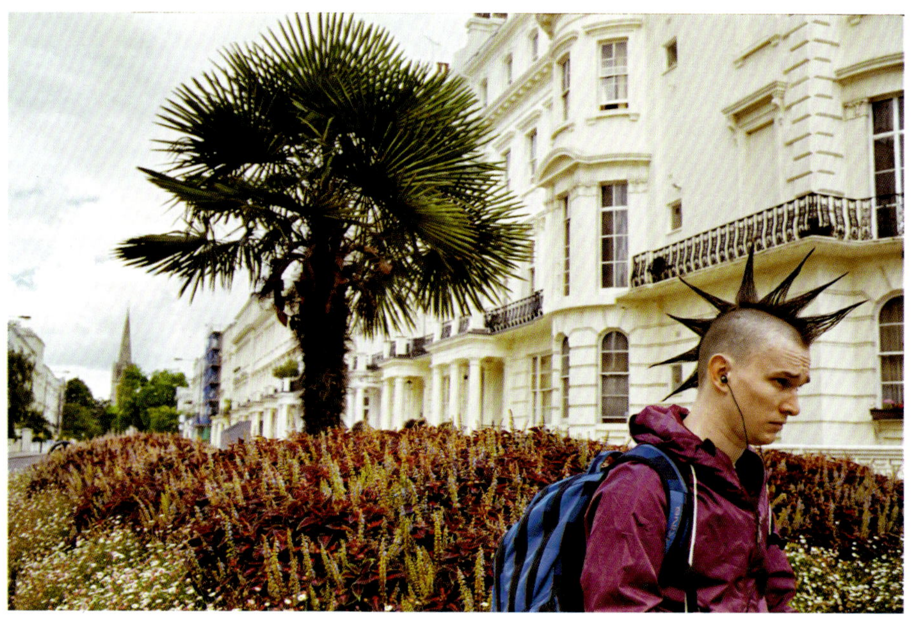

Kensington Park Road, London, 2014

Funny juxtapositions, visual wit, whatever you want to call it, street photography is awash with pictures that try to be funny or clever, or both. I hold my hands up – I've made pictures like this in my time. There's the peacock (pages 92–93), the man with his hair gelled into spikes, walking past a prickly-looking tree above, and the man with the advert pointing at his nose (opposite). People remember these images because they are compositionally strong, bold and engaging.

'Street photography is awash with pictures that try to be funny or clever, or both.'

With the peacock picture, the scene was set. I'd walked past the shop front for six months and photographed the peacock advert in many ways, but nothing had quite worked. One day, there in front of my shop was this colour-matching skip and I knew that was it. In many ways it was a simple shot to achieve – it's just two things next to each other and it needed to be taken straight on. What made it tricky was that people kept walking past and I wanted it to be free of pedestrians. I have lots of photos of that scene with people in, but none worked because the people were a distraction. Eventually I got the empty shot I wanted.

Be wary of taking a superior approach to your subject, which can result in mean, condescending pictures, rather than clever or funny ones. Respect your subject and the audience who might be looking at them.

While I'm all for embracing clichés, humour and wit, I advise a degree of

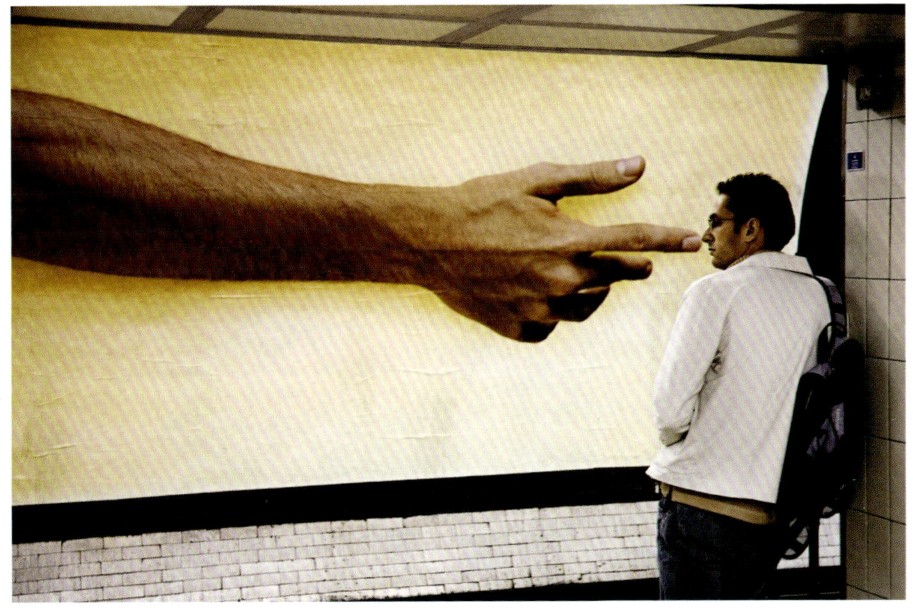

Moorgate Underground station, 2004

'Be wary of taking a superior approach to your subject, which can result in mean, condescending pictures.'

caution – beware the 'unfunny funnies'. The 'unfunny funny' is a picture that you think is funny, or a juxtaposition that you think is humorous, but isn't (or isn't any longer). It's a trope, something that's been done many times before, and you're just regurgitating it, badly. I'm all for visual gags and 'Ha ha, bonk!', but it has to be good.

TRY THIS

Check out how original your one-liner is at streetrepeat.org, an entertaining and eye-opening online collection of street photography's greatest repetitions.

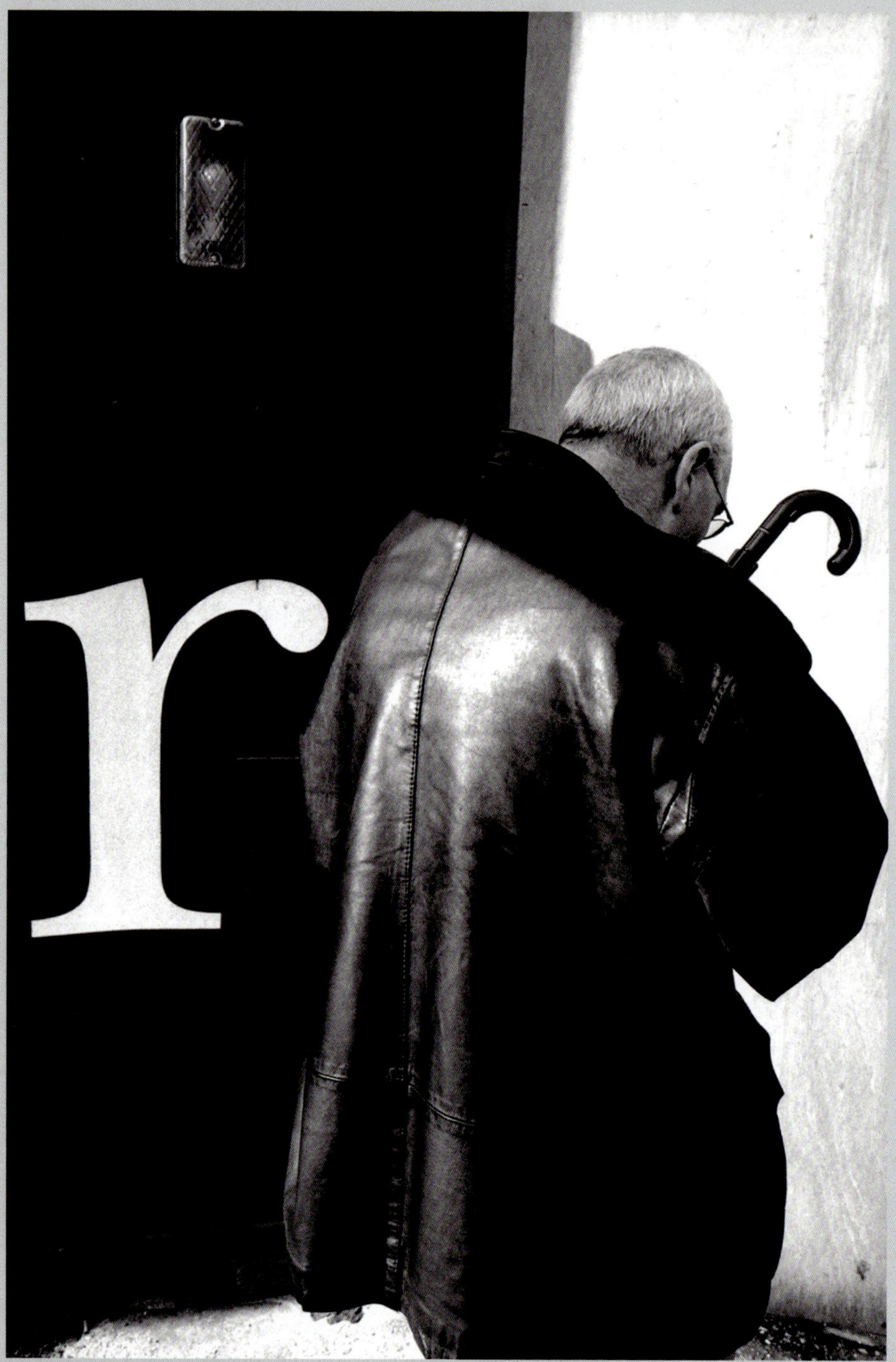

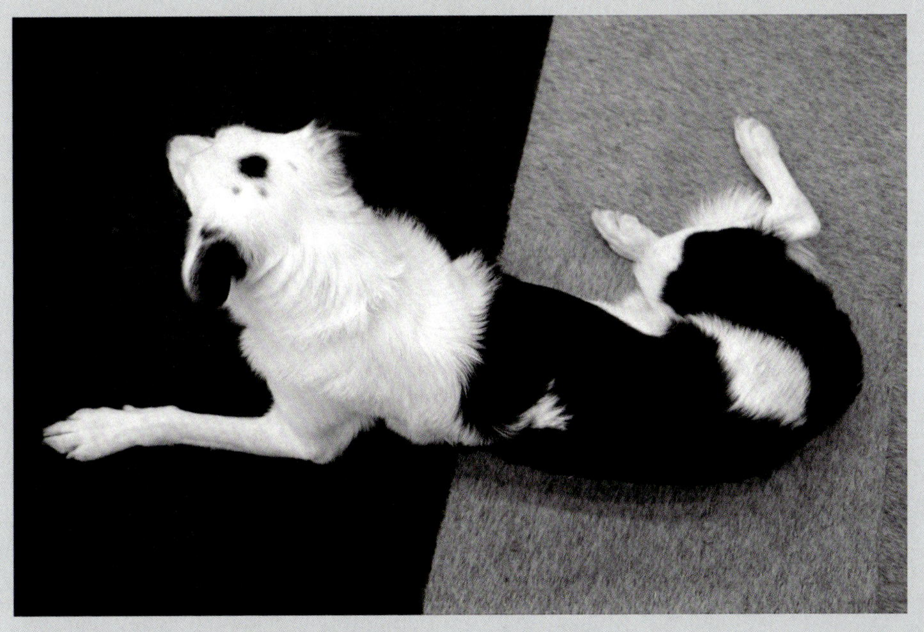

Opposite Paternoster Square, London, 2003   **Above** Earls Court, London, 2000

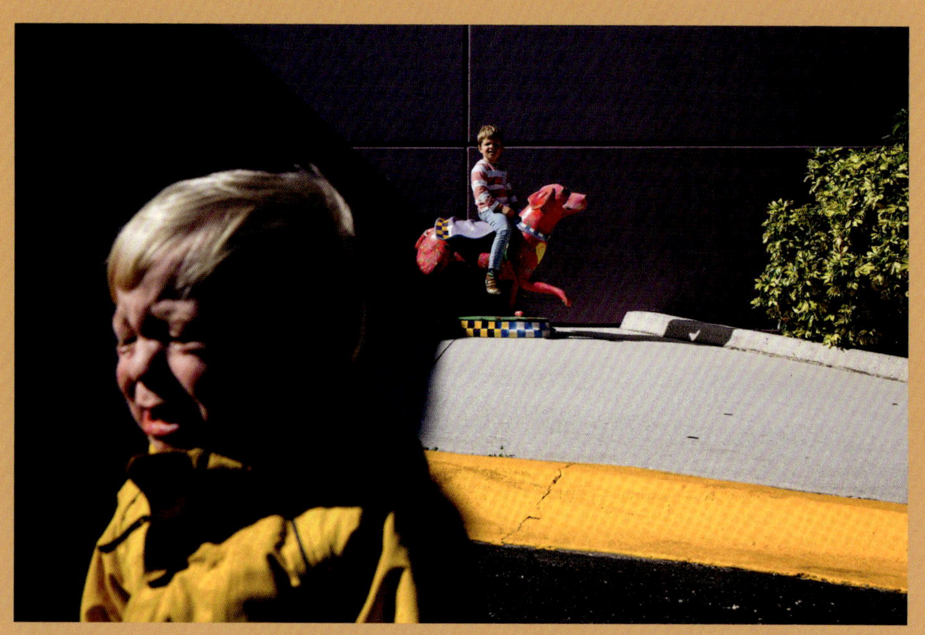

Florida, 2017

Chapter 16

ENGAGE AND REWARD

Hook the viewer
and keep them hooked

There are no rules when it comes to composition.
If you spot something that you think is interesting, photograph
it first, and only then think about how it might be part
of a bigger picture in which several things are going on.

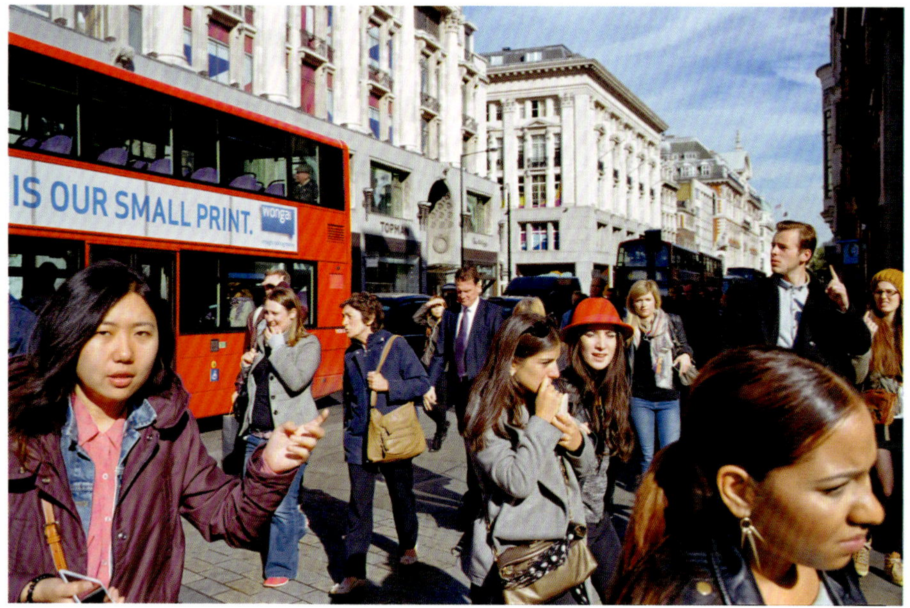

Oxford Circus, London, 2014

When it comes to composition, there is no right or wrong way, only different approaches – different strokes for different folks.

The quick catches, the pictures that hit you between the eyes, are among my favourite kinds of photograph – they make you feel that the photographer hadn't thought too much, even though he or she might well have.

Then there are the pictures that appear to be more considered and often feature many components stitched together. These images often arise from 'fishing'. If you spend time with the work of Alex Webb, Tony Ray-Jones and Lee Friedlander you'll see that their photographs not only engage, but also reward the more you look.

Take the image above, which I made in Oxford Circus. On the face of it, it's just an ordinary, busy street scene with people coming and going every which way.

There are lots of mini events within the whole. What I was looking for at the time is index fingers. There are seven index fingers being used in various ways. See if you can spot them. I also like how the colours go together nicely – there are flecks of purple, blue and red everywhere.

'When it comes to composition, there is no right or wrong, only different approaches – different strokes for different folks.'

With a picture such as this, where the action stretches across the entire frame, pay attention to what's happening at the edges as much as in the middle, because the edges help to pull everything together.

Photographer Cristóbal Hara is a master of the off-kilter composition. Sometimes it's worth standing back from a scene and trying to work out how you can f**k it up –

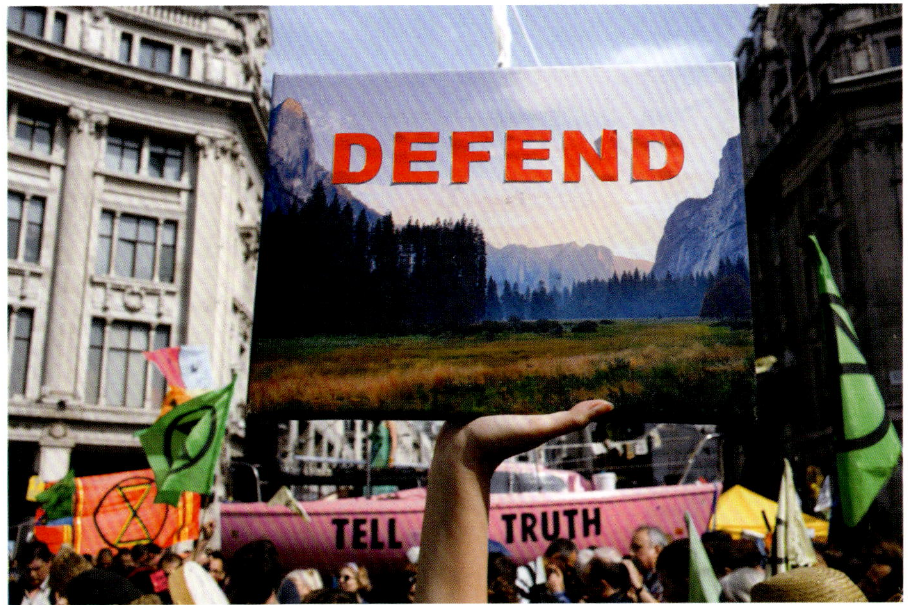

Oxford Circus, London, 2019

by which I mean, make the photograph more visually interesting rather than classically composed. That said, don't start obsessing over what you should or shouldn't do, or what other people have done, because you will drown in what's gone before. Everything has probably been photographed before; the question is whether *you* have seen and photographed it!

Whether you prefer the 'less is more' approach or like to compose images with multiple points of interest, do what feels right and be wary of imitating others. We all take inspiration from photographers who have gone before us or who are around today, and there's nothing wrong with that, but absorb it all and then make the pictures only you can make.

TRY THIS

Try 'rejecting' the main action
by putting it to the side of the frame.
Photographers are hard-wired to
shoot the main action at centre.
See if you can let that go.

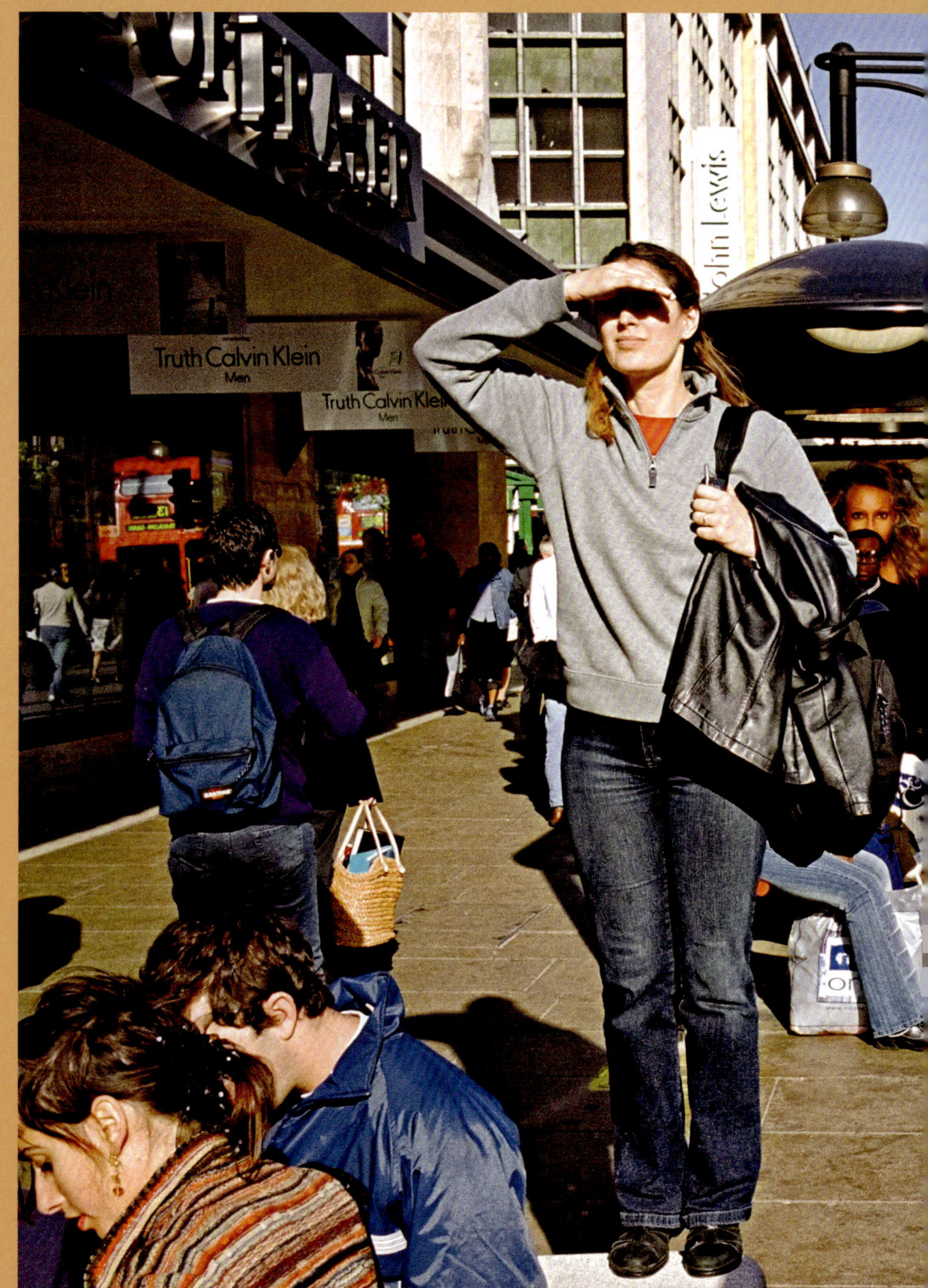

Oxford Street, London, 2004

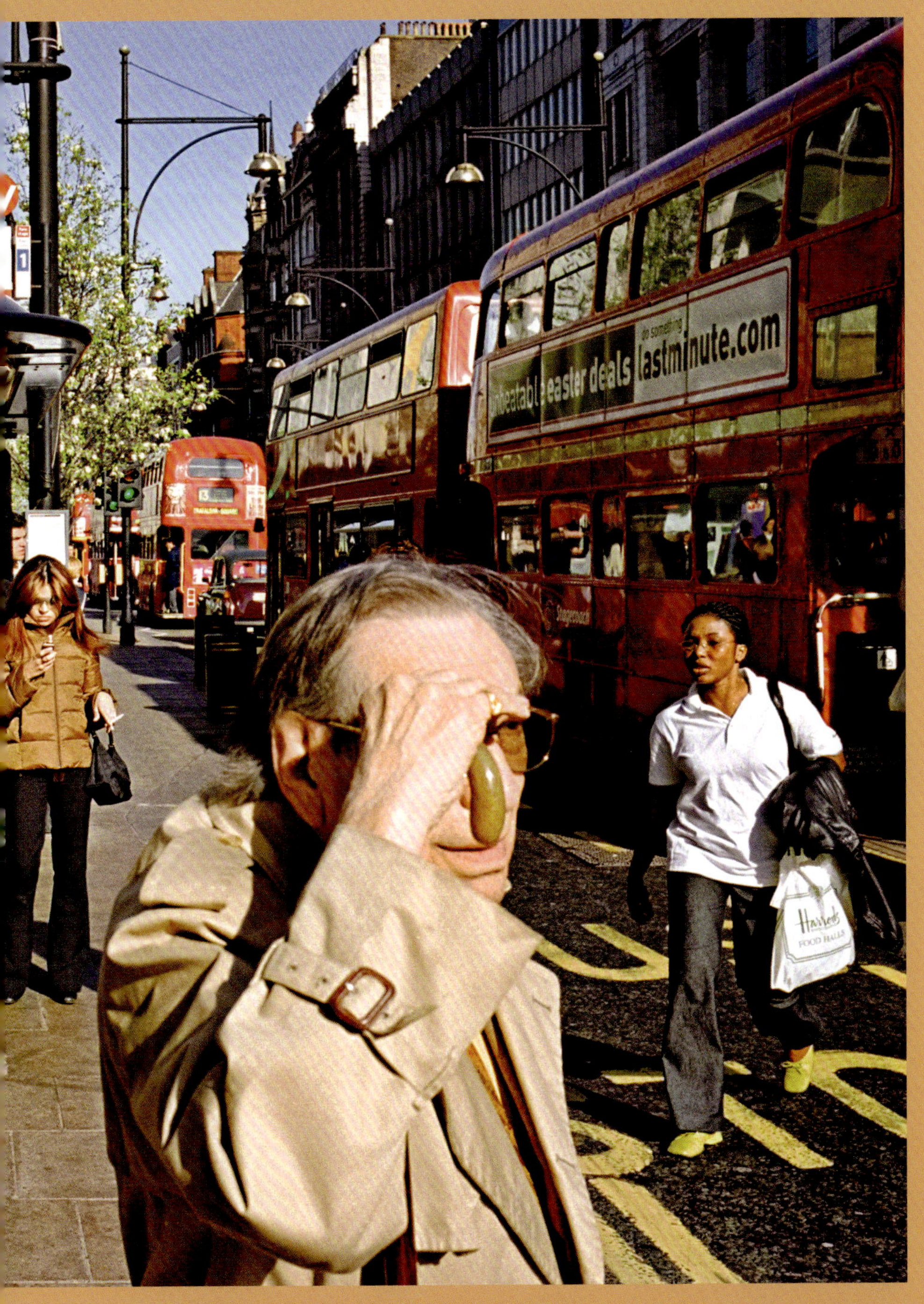

do something
unbeatabl easter deals lastminute.com
Stagecoach
13
TRAFALGAR SQUARE
Harrods
FOOD HALLS

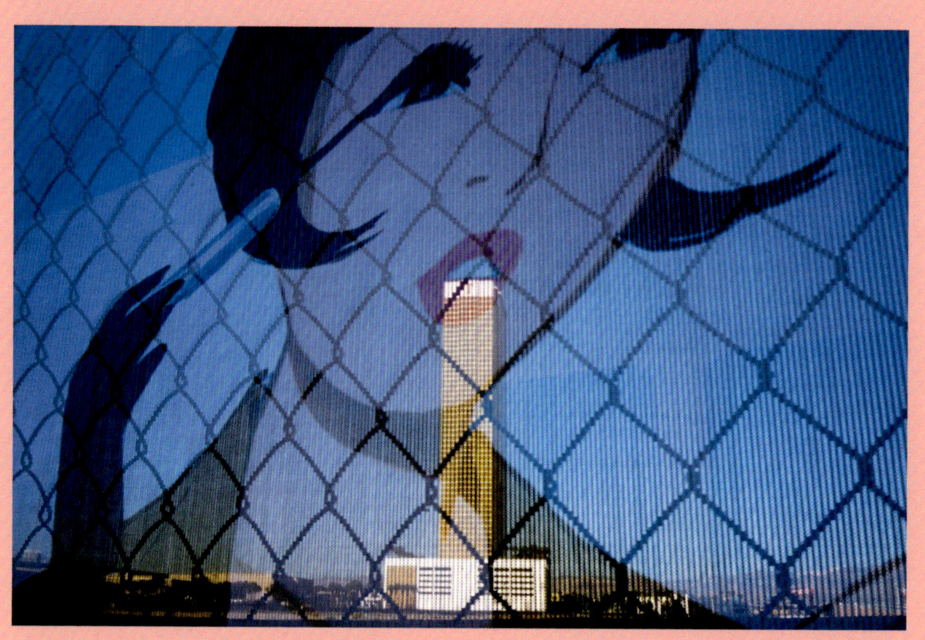

Las Vegas, 2017

Chapter 17

WHAT ABOUT HERE?

Get out of your comfort zone

Street photography is a frame of mind, a way of looking at things that can be applied to any situation, not just city streets. Venture into different environments, and be open to the opportunities that they might present.

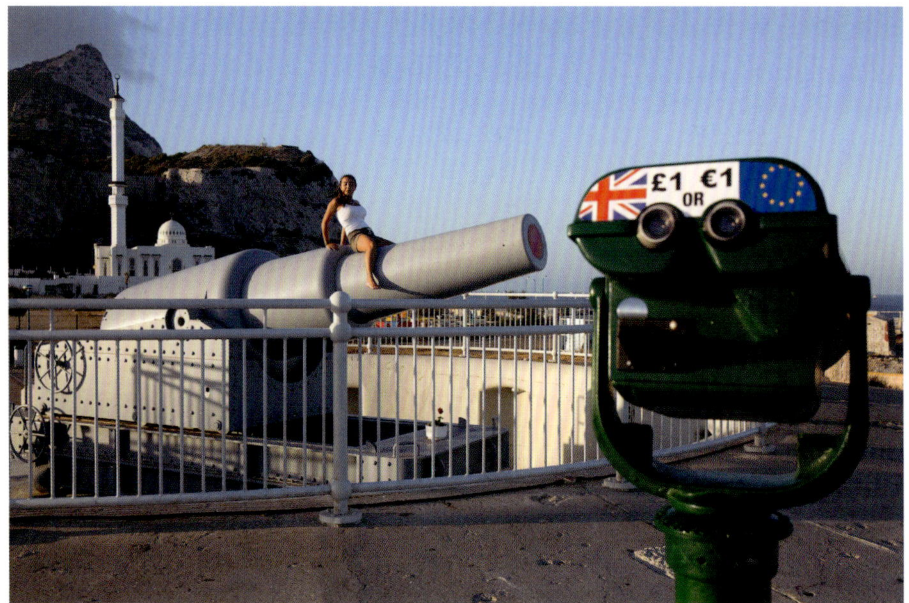

Gibraltar, 2017

Street photography is an attitude, a state of mind, a way of being, rather than something that has to be done exclusively on the streets of cities.

If you're truly a street photographer, you're a street photographer wherever you are in the world at any given moment. Although London has been my stomping ground for many years, I've never limited myself to just one city. I've frequently shot away from streets altogether and embraced locations in which it's more about the setting or mood than the constant flow of pedestrians.

The photograph on pages 108–09, taken in Gibraltar, doesn't have any people in it at all; there is only a monkey sitting in a window of a dilapidated building that looks out to sea, while on the grubby wall is a massive graffiti jellyfish.

I'm interested in making photographs that are relevant to the times, and over the last few years I've found I'm much more interested in photographing places that have a political edge. That said, I don't want to push my politics too much, although the President Trump image opposite is… well, you can make up your own mind. I want to make observations about what is happening in society at the moment because it is so interesting. I like that you can use photography to express something that is serious and political or comic and fun.

The image above, also taken in Gibraltar, is about as close as I will ever get to a one-frame Brexit image. I took it during the turmoil in the months after the UK narrowly voted to leave the European Union (EU), and I love the woman's smiley face and how this massive gun is pointing at the telescope, which has both the British and EU flags on it. I like it as an observation of a kind of happy moment before everything

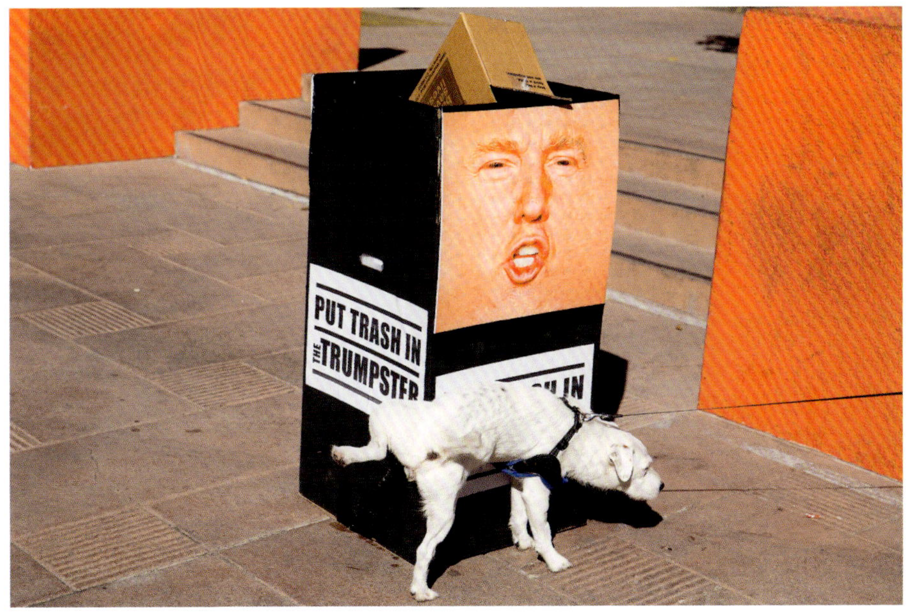

Pershing Square, Los Angeles, 2018

is blown to pieces, metaphorically speaking. It's an image that also plays with the gaze – the telescope resembles a strange, robot-like creature that looks back at us at the same time as looking out.

It's important, especially with countries or places that have a political edge to

'Street photography is an attitude, a state of mind, a way of being, rather than something that has to be done exclusively on the streets of cities.'

them, to work out where's hot and where's not. Just as in any city, the same suggestions apply about finding the right place, the right light, the right time of day, when's busy and when's not. When photographing somewhere new, first try to get a sense of the place by spending a few days exploring.

It's also wise to have an understanding of local customs, of what you should and shouldn't do. Being aware of what might cause offence will not only help to avoid social awkwardness, it will also give you confidence when you're out with your camera. If you know you're not doing anything wrong, you'll give off a good vibe and people will be less likely to bother you.

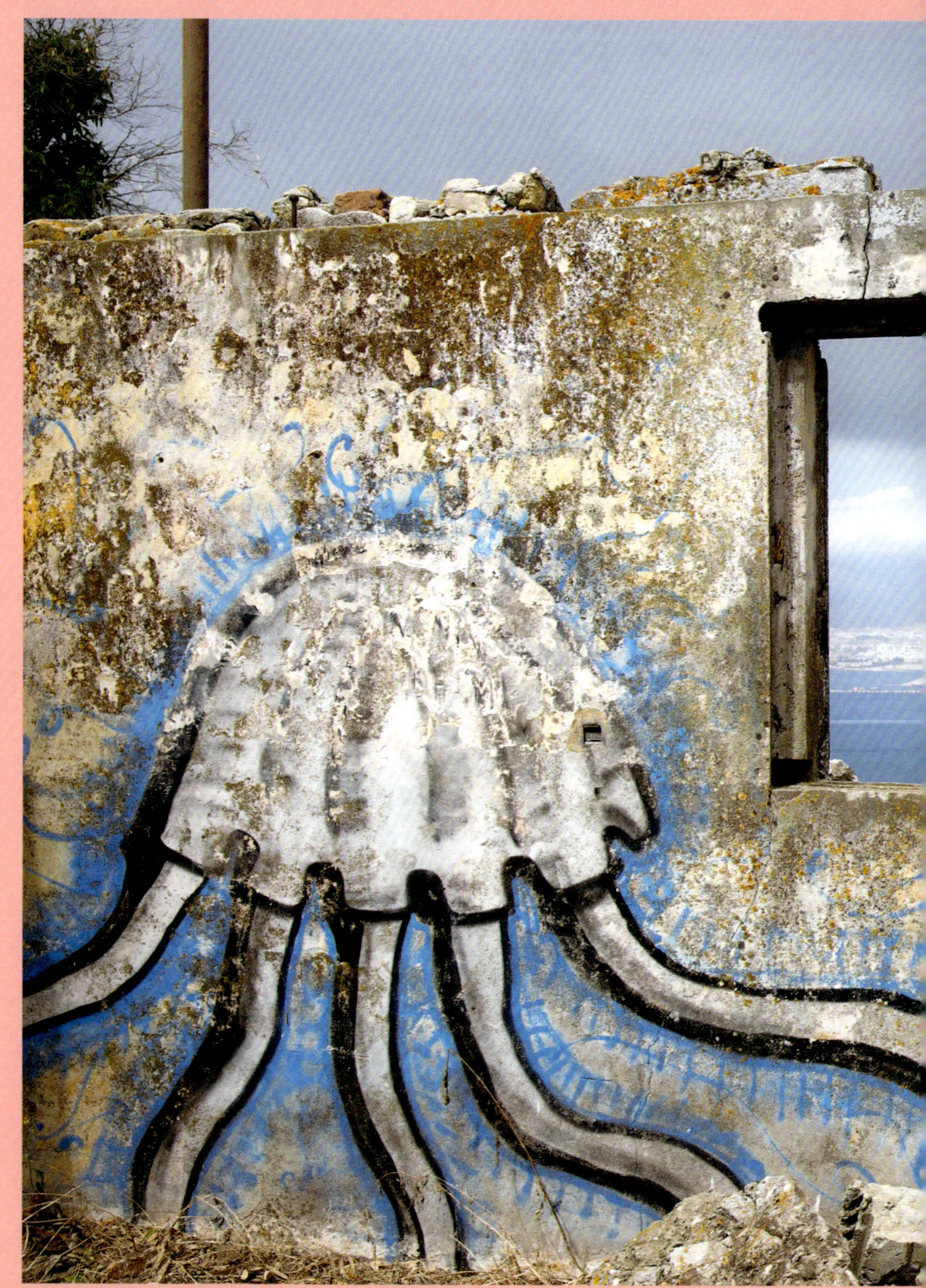

Gibraltar, 2017

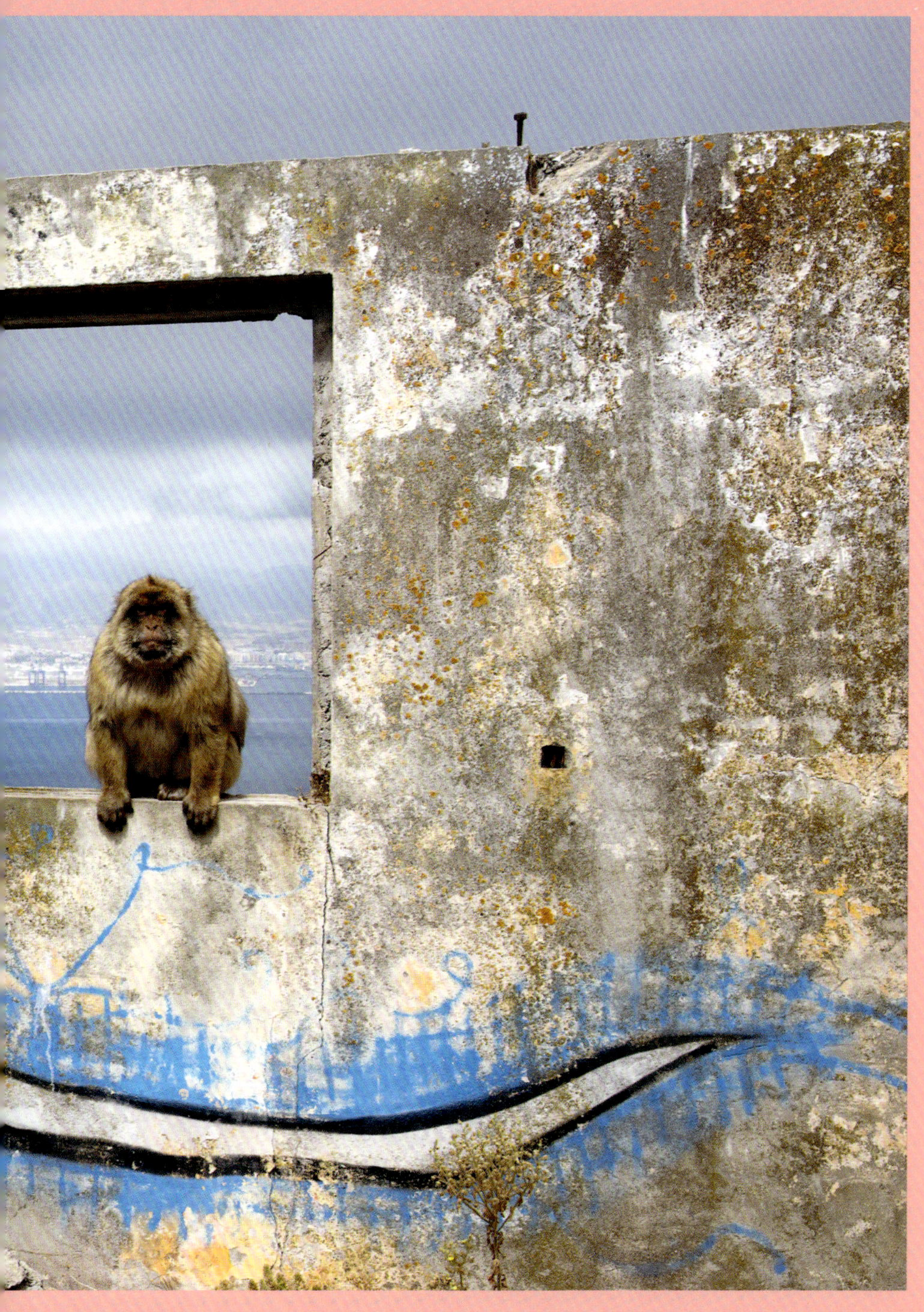

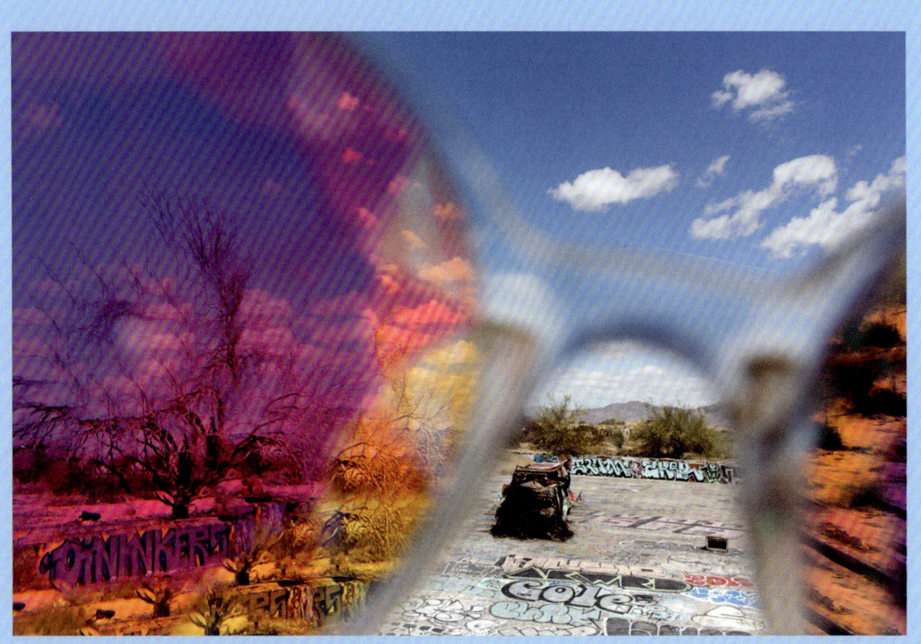

Slab City, California, 2018

Chapter 18

BROADEN YOUR HORIZONS

Be a street photographer wherever you are

You can fly halfway across the world, embed yourself in a completely alien setting and still make work that draws on the ethos and approaches of street photography.

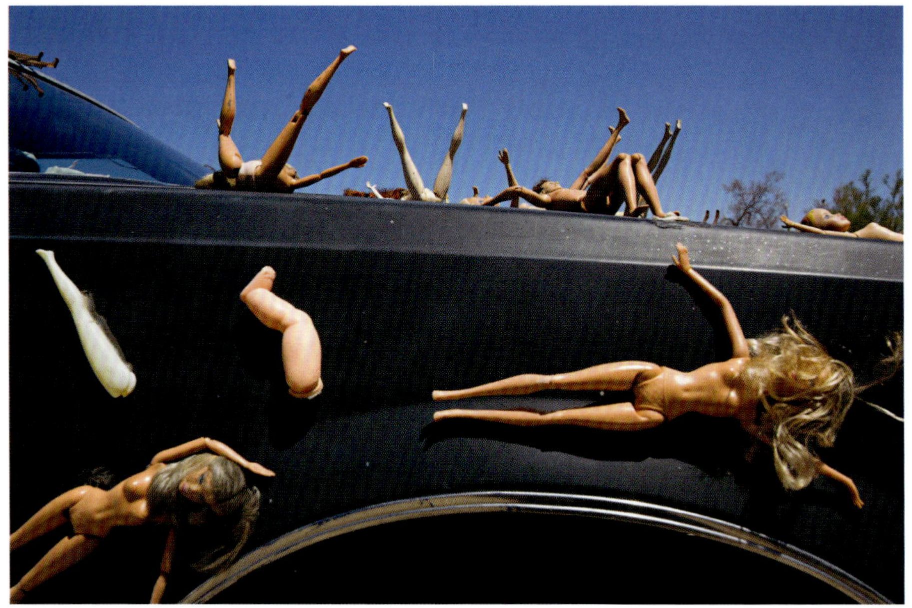

Slab City, 2018

My first love will always be street photography – pounding pavements for hours on end with my camera around my neck, scouring crowds for strange happenings. I make no bones that I do this for myself, not for anyone else. I don't feel under the same kind of pressure that a documentary or press photographer must be under, although I am, of course, fascinated by who, why and what we are.

> **'Shooting… away from conventional city streets, becomes more about people and place, almost in a documentary sense.'**

My curiosity about people is the driving force behind why I make pictures in a traditional street-photography sense. It's also what led me to travel all the way to southern California's Sonoran Desert, where I made my project 'Slab City'.

Built by the US military as barracks for the Marine Corps in 1942, the compound is a self-proclaimed city, but in reality, it's an extremely hot (38°C/100°F) squatter camp. People roam around as they do in a conventional city or town, but because it's so small, you get to know everyone. I certainly did anyway because I'm gregarious and wanted to meet the people who call this place home.

Shooting in a place like Slab City, away from conventional city streets, becomes more about people and place, almost in a documentary sense. Although I was capturing spontaneous moments, I was able to forge a deeper connection with my subjects because I was there for a long period of time – about four weeks – staying in my camper van. I made portraits of residents in the landscape and photographed

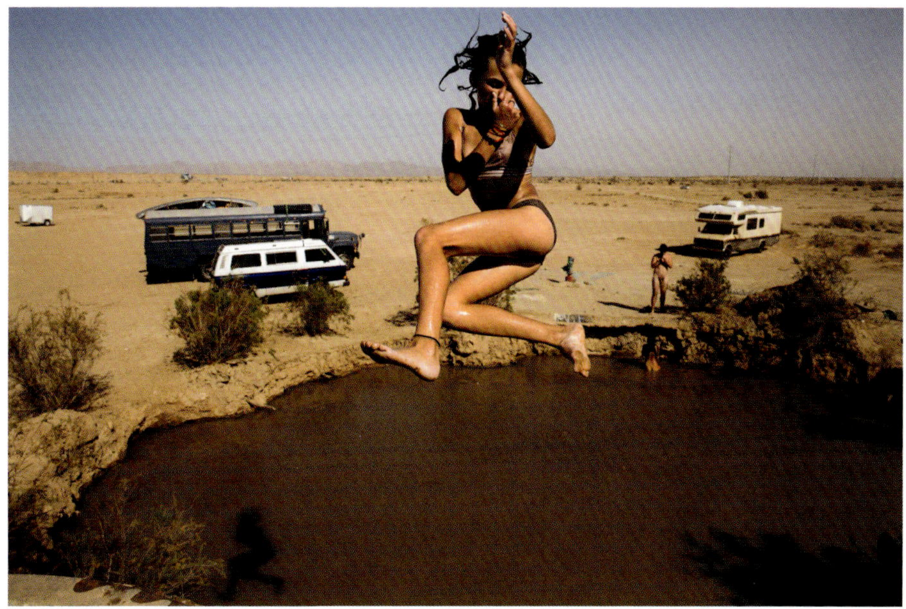

Slab City, 2018

the setting itself, as well as taking candid shots like the image above of a girl jumping into a big mud pool, which was a captured moment just as in street photography.

Making the work became, in a sense, about embracing a documentary approach, but retaining a street-photographer mentality – always looking for things, being eagle-eyed, reacting quickly.

I found Slab City to be a strange place. There is no proper water supply, electricity or sanitation. It's very anarchic and quite dangerous, but also very interesting. Street photography is fantastic, but the relationships you have with people are generally fleeting. You look at them, find them attractive in some way, make the picture, and move on. On this trip I was interested in spending time with the people I met and getting to understand them. I wanted to take pictures in the same way as on the street, but

with a little more insight. In any case, I couldn't have just turned up and started photographing without introducing myself. It wouldn't have gone down

'It is possible to take some of the ways of working as a street photographer and apply them to completely different environments.'

well. There were a few days when I didn't even pick up my camera – I just got to know the residents.

The point I'm trying to make is that it is possible to take some of the ways of working as a street photographer and apply them to completely different environments. Street photography is about showing people and places, and you can do that anywhere, even if there aren't any pavements in sight.

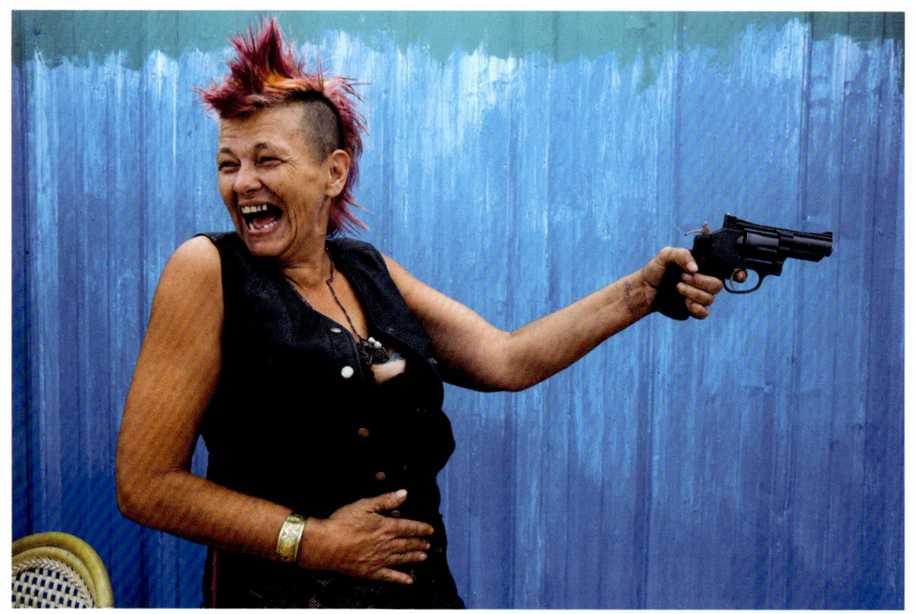

Slab City, 2018

TRY THIS

Photograph your family candidly,
like a street photographer. Show the
tears, falls, accidents and upsets
as well as the triumphs and joys.

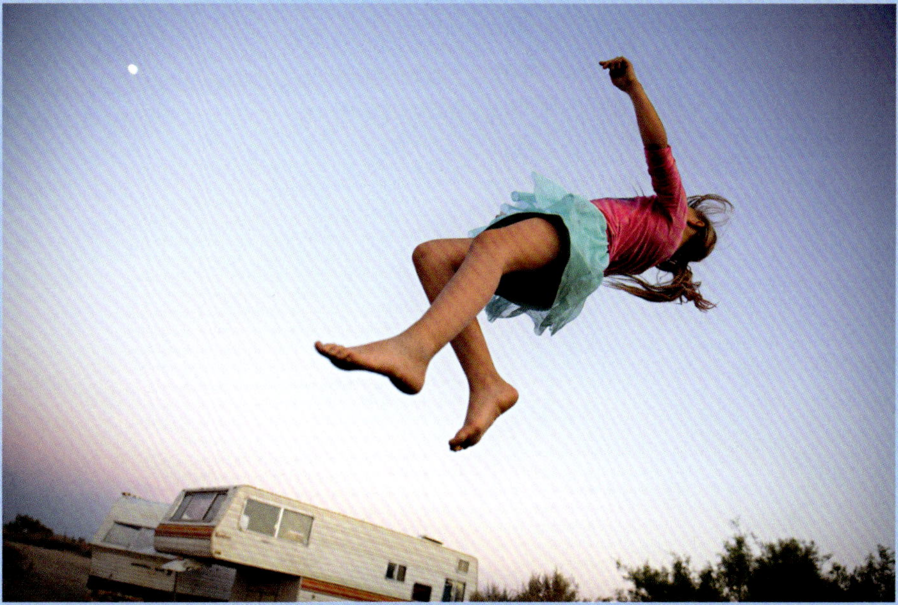

Slab City, 2018

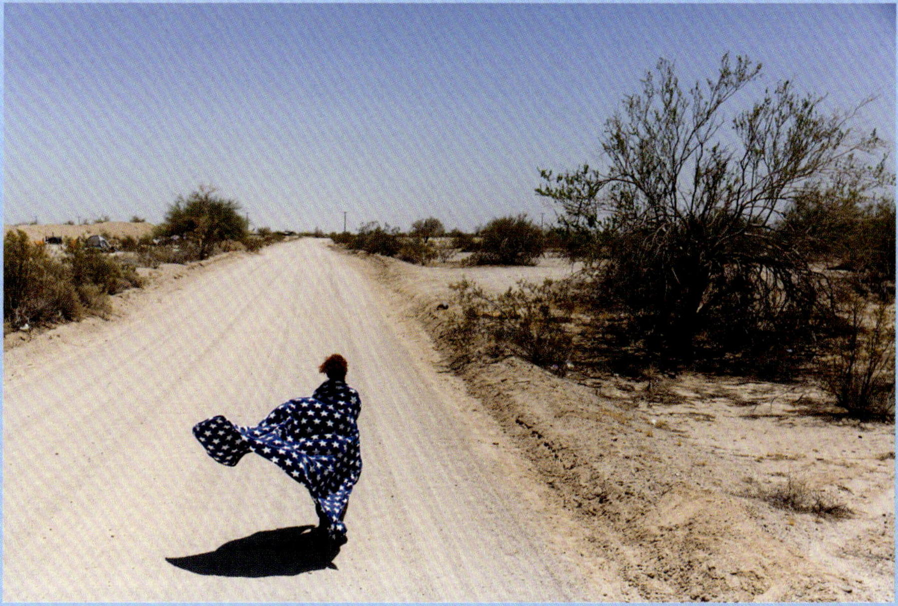

Slab City, 2018

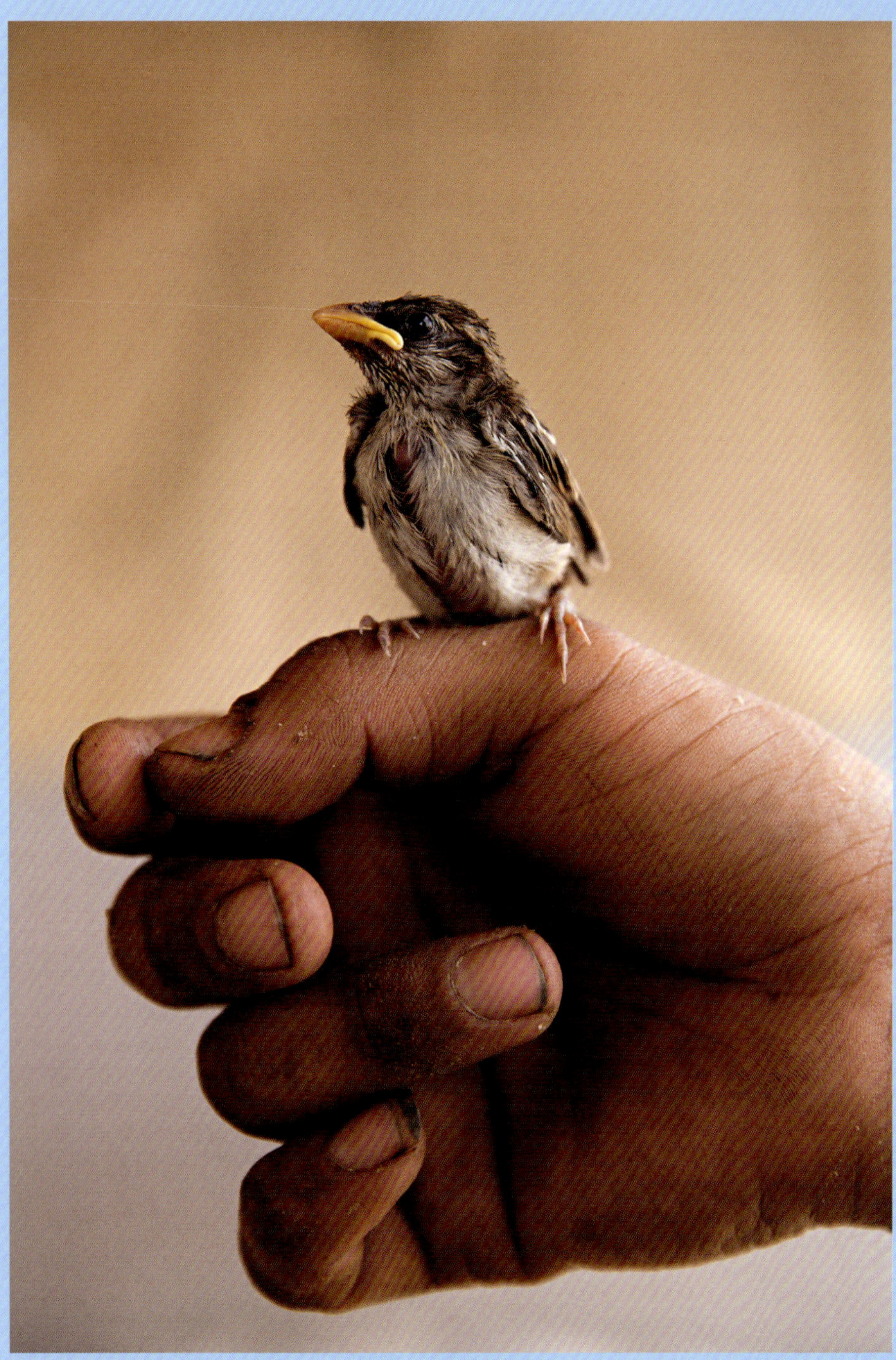

Slab City, 2018

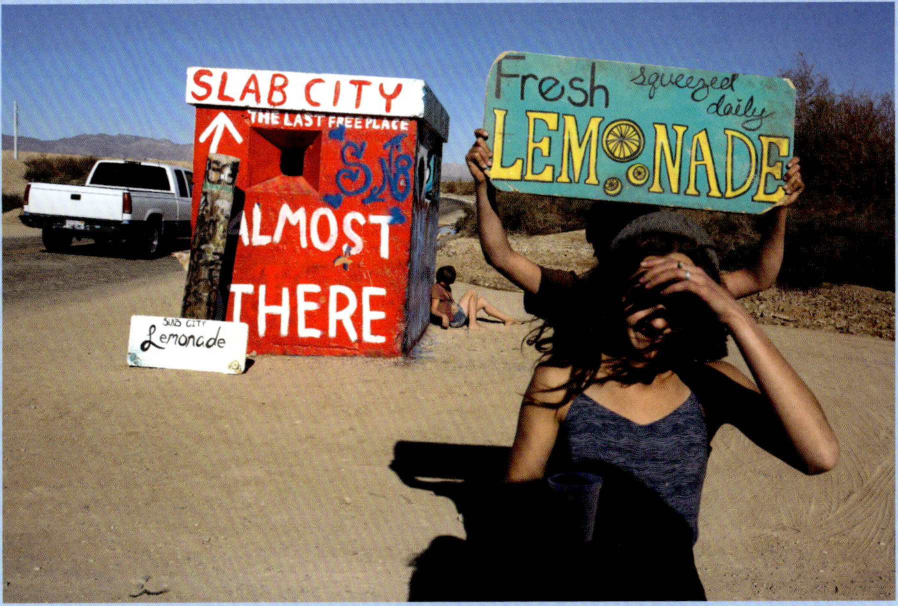

Slab City, 2018

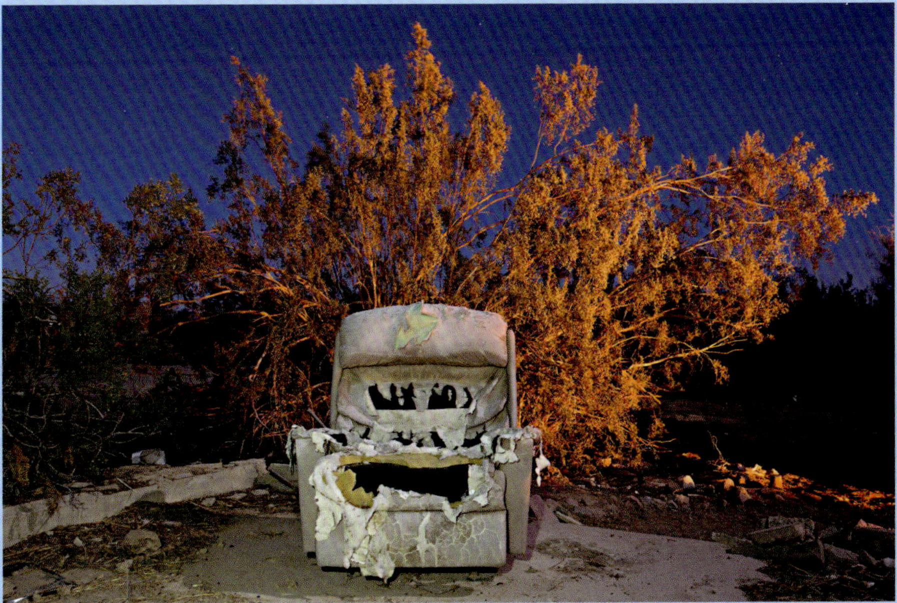

Slab City, 2018

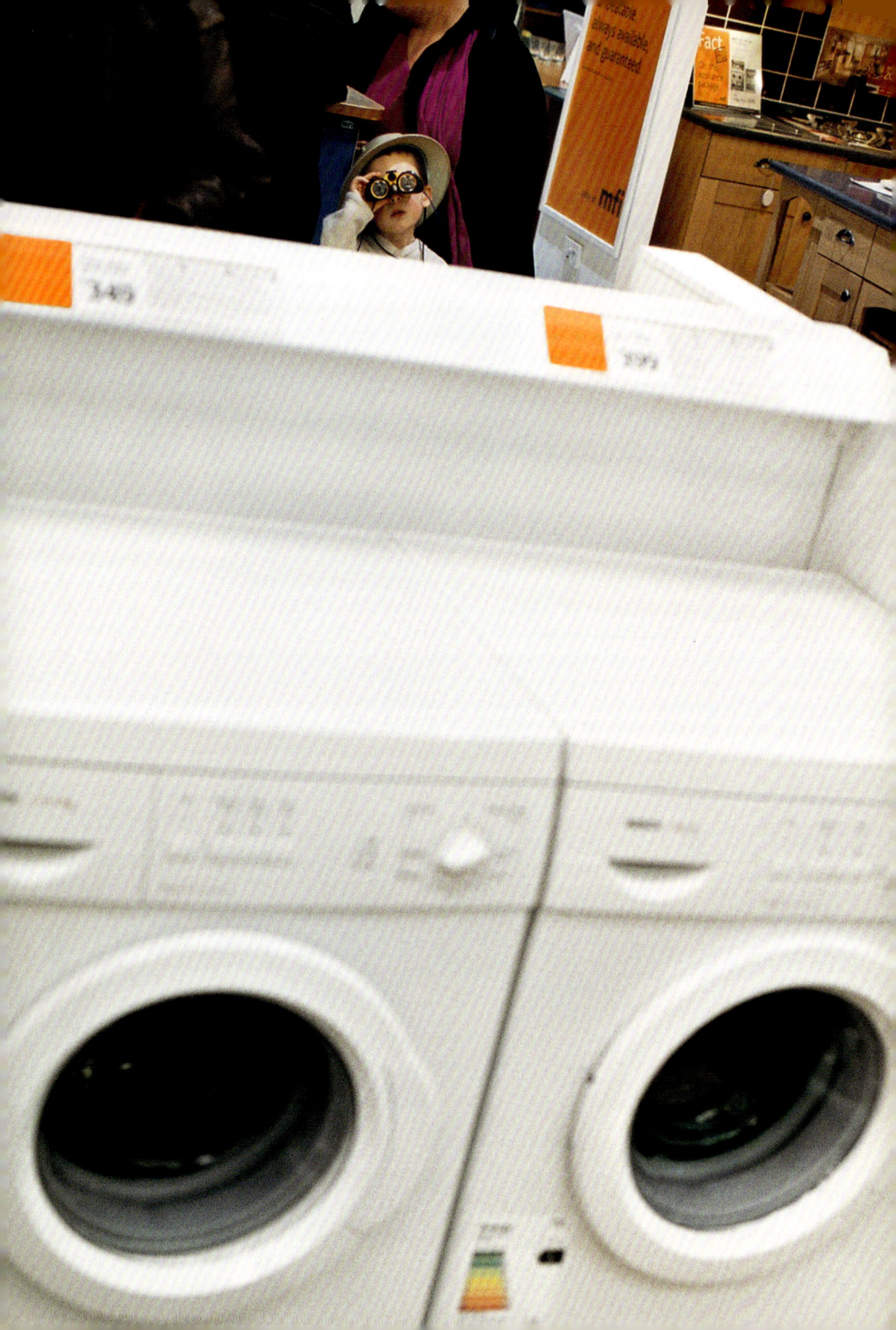
always available
and guaranteed
Fact
mfi

OWN YOUR VISION

All moments are undecided and indecisive... until you edit

It's vital to find a way to make sense of your pictures, and how they work with each other. You can find links – even if only tenuous or jarring – through sequencing.

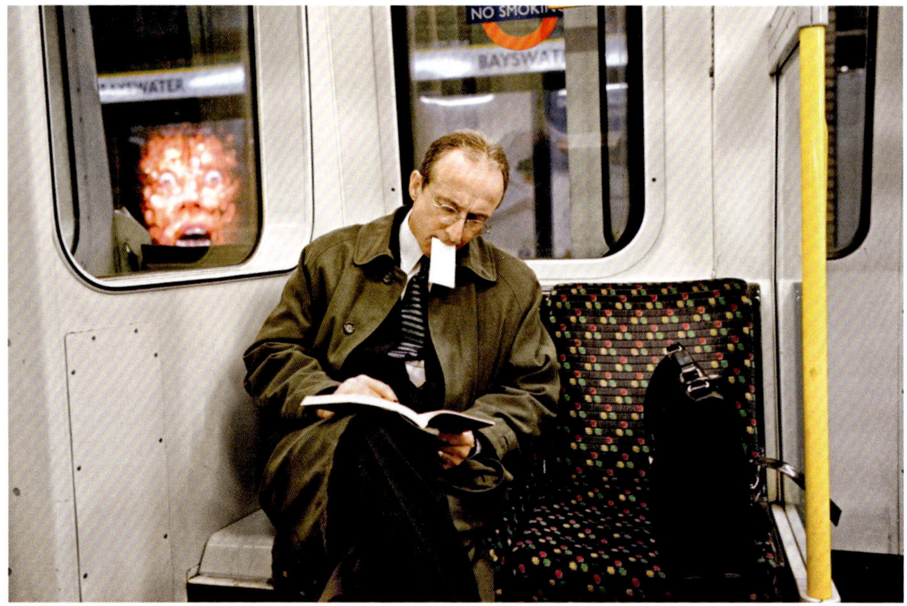

Page 118 Luton, 2002   Above Bayswater Underground station, London, 2004

f street photography is about single, unrelated images, how do you choose the 'best' shots and create compelling sequences? I'm the first to admit this is a time-consuming Rubik's Cube of an undertaking for which there is no universal foolproof method.

When I made my book *All That Life Can Afford* (2016) with book designer and editor Stuart Smith, I spent two years agonizing over which images should go where. I'd pair pictures that seemed to work well together and then sleep on it, only to realize the next day that it didn't work. I wanted to ensure that each image was in the book because it was a strong image in its own right, but felt it was also crucial to create conversations between images if the book was to be a success.

One of the things I learned from Stuart is that the first picture should lead the viewer into the rest of the book. Incidentally, the following advice applies to any edit you might be working on: start strong and finish strong. This is to do with something called the primacy and recency effect, which refers to people's tendency to most easily recall the first and last items in a list and forget those in the middle.

'The following advice applies to any edit you might be working on: start strong and finish strong.'

If you look at this as a graph, you'll see it's like a smile – high at the start, dipping in the middle and high at the end. You can apply the same logic to a sequence of images: since those at the start and end are more likely to remain in people's minds, you should make sure they're good ones. This is the key, in my opinion, to any good edit.

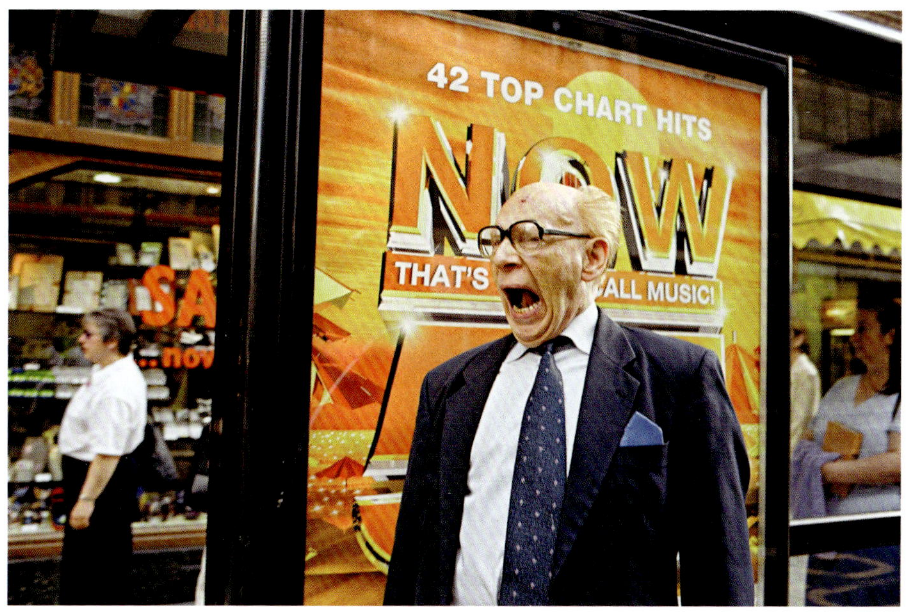

High Holborn, 2003

I find there is only one way to edit and that is by printing out your images and re-ordering them on the floor, wall or table. If you think you can edit on a computer, you are fooling yourself. You need to physically move the images around, touch them, put them next to each other, and even put them over each other. This is because, in a book, one page leads to the next page and the 'warmth' of one image 'soaks through' to the next one, leaving its mark on the following page like an imprint or an echo.

Stuart and I used different criteria to link images, from colour and shapes to the weather and gestures. I think of these sequences as sentences or phrases. You might get a run of four images linked by a certain gesture, and then a 'break' where an image with no obvious link to the one before it momentarily interrupts the flow. A break serves as a brief pause for breath, as in a piece of music. And then you start again. You're looking for all kinds of linking devices that smooth the transition from one image to the next, or

'You need to physically move the images around, touch them, put them next to each other...'

purposefully jar it. Some might be subtle, others more obvious, some complete lunacy, but the only thing that matters is that they make sense to you. Some people give the impression that there is a mystique surrounding the editing process, an assumption that it's some kind of magical art, but that really isn't so.

Here's an example. The link between the images opposite and above is quite explicit – you have a scared face and a scary face. Another example is the link between the pictures overleaf – the

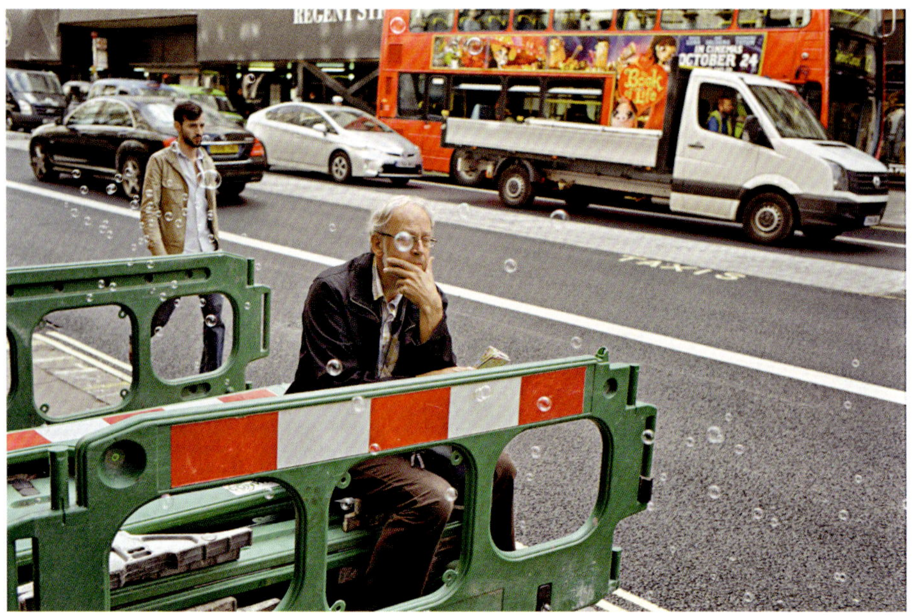

Regent Street, London, 2014

man with a bubble over his eye and the three women wearing wigs. The red is an obvious link, and the circles resonate

'Some people give the impression that there is a mystique surrounding the editing process… that it's some kind of magical art, but that really isn't so.'

from one image to the next, the discs in the window display echoing the bubbles. You can have a lot of fun with this.

Just a brief word of warning: beware of editing in a way that patronizes the viewer by stating the obvious: 'Oh look, there's a person lying down and someone else doing the same in the next image!' It's not just about matching up similar things. Sequencing pictures can be far more cerebral than simply colour matching or playing snap. Sometimes there is

something intangible in a picture that makes sense going into the next, and that's just as valid as a repeated shape. In fact, there's something quite intangible about editing full stop. It's almost a case of letting the edit, or sequencing, take shape organically and resisting the temptation to shoehorn your pictures into a pre-imagined concept.

So for any edit you're working on – whether for a website, Instagram feed, book or exhibition – always ask, 'Why is that picture next to that one?' And revise, revise, revise until it feels right.

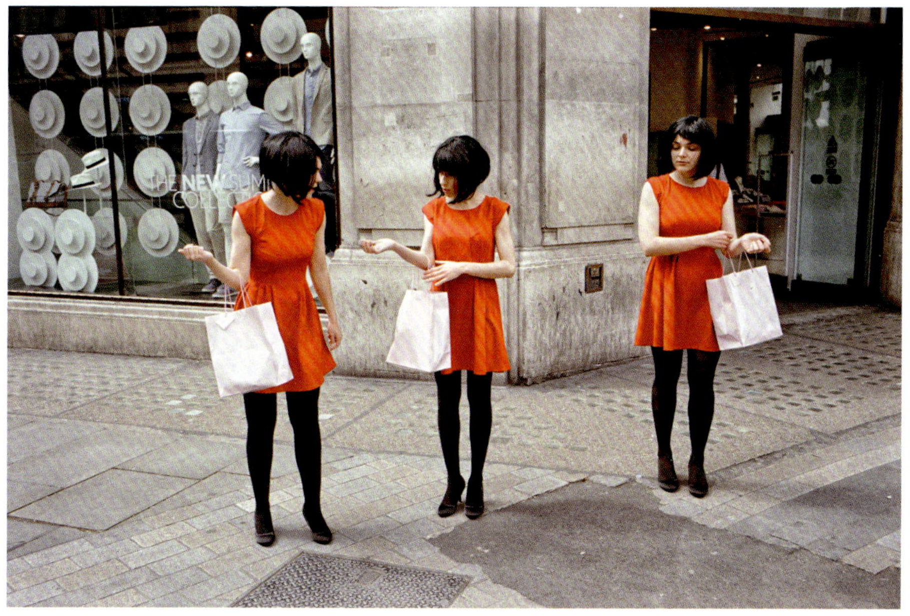

Regent Street, London, 2014

TRY THIS

Print your photos out. Try sequencing them by colour, weather, shape, size of subject, location and time of day. See what happens when you edit with each criterion.

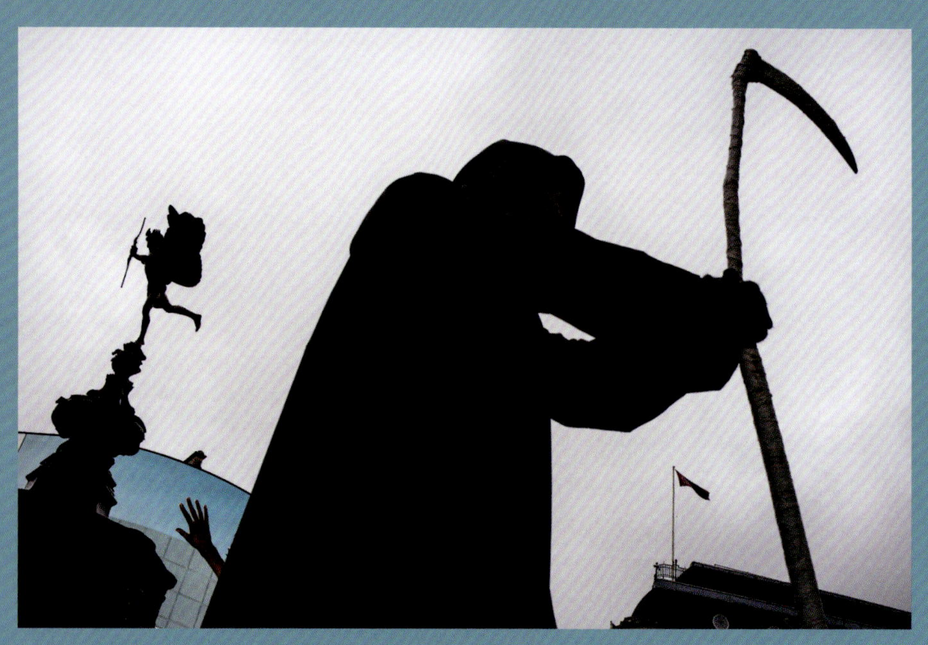

Chapter 20

THE LAST WORD

Keep the faith –
and see you on the street!

If you're serious about making pictures, you have
to keep going and strive to be better. The only
limitations are those you place on yourself.

Let's not beat around the bush. Street photography isn't easy. A walk in the park it is not. But when it works, when the stars align, there is nothing else quite like it. And it is for those moments we as photographers live.

If you're serious about making pictures, if this is really what you want to do, you have to keep going and keep striving to be better. Don't look for excuses or create barriers for yourself; don't succumb to self-doubt or fear. The only limitations are those you place on yourself. If you're going to go into this big wide world with your camera, where you don't know what's going to happen and you don't know what you're going to photograph, you may as well be open to anything and roll with the punches.

'If you're really serious about making pictures... keep going and keep striving to be better... Don't look for excuses or create barriers for yourself.'

Don't listen to the naysayers who claim that street photography has had its day, or that it's all been done before, or that there's no point doing it because everyone is taking pictures now since everyone has a camera on their phone, and it's with them at all times. There will always be a place for street photography, for great seeing and recording of life, because the end result is so vital and life-affirming: it is a way of understanding ourselves as human beings. John Szarkowski wrote of fellow photographer Garry Winogrand that his ambition 'was not to make good pictures, but through photography to know life'.

We do need to keep pushing for fresh thinking in street photography, which demands fresh seeing and that we don't just churn out the same old stuff. So forget everything you've seen and know, and concentrate on what you *feel*. Once you open yourself up to that and give yourself permission to be at one with the street, everything will come alive and you'll start to see pictures everywhere that represent you and your feelings, whether they are happy or sad, even if they are a reflection through other people.

As I said at the beginning of this book, it's a privilege to be making street photography. A camera is an invitation to be more involved in what's going on, to get closer, which is why people enjoy making pictures – it's a reason for being somewhere, or just a reason for being.

If I knew the perfect way to make a great street photograph, I would tell you, but the truth is, I don't know. I can only share what I feel, think and do, which is what I hope has been achieved in these pages.

What keeps me doing this? The constant discovery. Primarily, it's because I enjoy being out and about. I'm interested in *how* we are and *what* we do. I'm nosy, curious and I like both looking at people existing and thinking about what it means to exist; I'm an existentialist.

It also keeps me pretty healthy. I go out and walk around all day, most days. I don't sit at a desk. I occasionally do commissioned work, but really, I do whatever I can to make a living, including selling pictures and running workshops. Doing this is definitely not going to make you rich financially, but it can make you rich spiritually (eye roll!). To go out and feel things about people and try to capture those things is not a bad way to spend your days. Physically and mentally, I think it's very healthy. Street photography helps me think not only about how we as humans respond to things, but also about how I respond

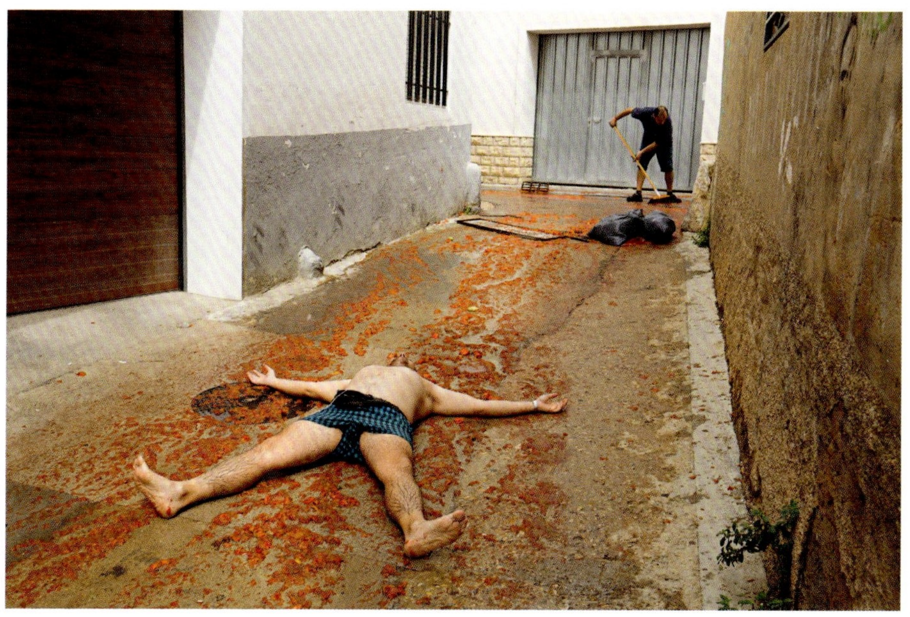

Page 124 Piccadilly Circus, London, 2018 **Above** Buñol, Spain, 2017

to things – how do I deal with this when that happens, how do I deal with that when this happens? I learn from it. I put myself in situations I find challenging, or that provoke a range of emotions, and try to examine how I feel about things.

'If you're going to go into this big wide world with your camera... you may as well be open to anything and roll with the punches.'

Ultimately, you're doing this for yourself, so if you're doing it for anyone else, you're starting off on the wrong foot.

I love making pictures, particularly the act of photographing. The engagement, the feeling, the being involved is far more important to me than the 'getting'. If the picture is good, it's a bonus. If it's not, c'est la vie. The enjoy-ment of photographing is a hundred times more rewarding than the photograph itself. So buy a good pair of comfortable shoes, have a camera around your neck at all times, keep your elbows in, be patient, optimistic, and don't forget to smile.

ACKNOWLEDGEMENTS

I would like to thank the following people: my partner, Suzanne, for her love, enthusiasm and for putting up with me; my parents David and Susan, and brother Adam, who are my greatest admirers and critics; Gemma Padley, photography writer and editor, who patiently turned my words into writing; John Parton, commissioning editor at Laurence King, who came up with the book idea; Blanche Craig, senior editor, who orchestrated everything; Derren Brown, magician and street photographer, for his encouraging and enthusiastic foreword; Blake Andrews, Narelle Autio, Jared Iorio, Richard Kalvar, Jesse Marlow, Joel Meyerowitz, Cole Orloff, Trent Parke, Martin Parr, Gus Powell for their friendship and counsel.

And finally, my thanks to Leica cameras for their unwavering support and incredible cameras.

Matt Stuart uses the Leica M system, usually with a 35 mm lens.

ABOUT THE AUTHOR

Matt Stuart has always enjoyed observing people, much to the frustration of his teachers and employers, who found his attention was often elsewhere. Then he discovered photography in his early twenties, which allowed him to choose his own subjects and make his own decisions. Since that time he has been in constant demand by clients and photographers around the world, who enjoy his genuine take on life, via his online commentary, books, exhibitions and inspirational workshops.

His humour and generosity to other photographers is always evident. His first book, *All That Life Can Afford* (2016), shows the photographic results of having lived and worked in London for 20 years. His second book *Into the Fire* (2020) is a portrait of an off-the-grid camp called 'Slab City' based in the Sonoran desert in California. *Think Like a Street Photographer* explains to readers how to go about developing the attitude and persistence necessary to capture extraordinary photographs.

Matt lives in The Netherlands with his Dutch partner, Suzanne, and has three – sons Oscar, Max and Felix.

www.mattstuart.com
www.instagram.com/mattu1/
www.mapsimages.com